THINGS TO DO

WITH

TODDLERS AND

TWOS

THINGS TO DO

WITH

TODDLERS AND TWOS

NEW AND REVISED EDITION

Written and illustrated by

Karen Miller

Telshare Publishing Co., Inc.

International Standard Book Number: 0-910287-15-5

Library of Congress Card Number: 00-105250

NEW AND REVISED EDITION

Third Printing: January 2005

DEDICATION

An inspiring keynote speaker, Dr. Grace Mitchell rarely addressed a large audience without receiving a standing ovation. She challenged adults to live up to their highest potential. "Do something, no matter how small, right away, that will help set your feet on the track to change your life. Order that college catalog, call the number of that weight loss program, take that class." Her most important message was that we should never stop learning and stretching our awareness. Grace showed us a sense of mission and a *style of being.* She was fond of saying, "When I wake up each morning I ask myself, 'I wonder what wonderful thing is in store for me today?' By the time I go to bed, I can always point to some happening."

A pioneer in our field, Grace Mitchell started her Green Acres Nursery School and Day Camp near Boston in 1940. She went on to found the Living and Learning Centres in the Northeast, and served the profession as a governing board member of NAEYC. She wrote several books along the way, started her own publishing company, and lectured widely. Considerable though her professional accomplishments were, she is admired most for her model of personal growth. She earned her master's degree from Harvard at the age of 53 and her Ph.D. at age 70!

Her favorite metaphor was "ripples." A leader of a large, high-quality child care organization once told me, "When I was just out of college I was much influenced by a woman who had been a center director for Grace Mitchell...so, of course, she was wonderful!" Dr. Mitchell reminded people that the impact of their actions does not stop with those they contact directly. "Like throwing a pebble in a pond," she said, "the ripples go out from one small action and you never know how far they will reach."

Dr. Grace Mitchell died on January 27, 2000, just two weeks after her 91st birthday. Some people you meet in life go in and out of your awareness quickly. But no one who has ever gotten to know Grace, has heard her speak, or who has even had a casual conversation with her will forget her. May we make big "ripples" to honor her!

ACKNOWLEDGMENTS

The seeds for this book were planted when I was asked to present a workshop on curriculum for toddlers at a conference of the Colorado Association for the Education of Young Children in 1983. I immediately called my friend and respected colleague, Jo Layfield. We spent two weekends brainstorming at Jo's cabin in the mountains and the resulting workshop handout became the outline for this book. I thank Jo for her many pragmatic ideas and her "catalytic action."

As this revised edition takes shape 18 years later, I see in front of me the faces of many hundreds of caregivers and directors – people I have visited and observed in their child care centers and family child care programs, and those who have generously shared their ideas, questions and concerns at workshops I have presented. It is these people who have anchored me in reality. I am particularly grateful to Laurene Ellmers Phillips and the staff of her toddler center, The Elm Tree in Boulder, Colorado, where I have spent time renewing my exposure to toddlers and found many fine examples of good language and sensitive interactions of staff with children.

The editing skill of Lois Dewsnap, the production abilities of Don Dewsnap, and the skillful management of Telshare's president, Nancy Bailey, are prime factors in the ongoing success of this book. It was the interest and constant encouragement of Dr Grace Mitchell and her willingness to publish this author's first book through her Telshare Publishing Company that really made the whole thing happen.

CONTENTS

PART TWO – ACTIVITIES

Chapter 4: Chanting, Naming, Listening, Talking   55

Chapter 10: Splashing and Playing with Water   **133**

Chapter 11: Touching, Tasting, Smelling, Looking –
Sensory Play   **141**

Chapter 12: Moving   **163**

Chapter 15: Making Friends   **195**

INTRODUCTION

Toddlers are learners. They seem to spend every waking moment trying to figure out how the world works. As they develop new skills like climbing or walking, they have to find out just how far that skill will take them, and practice it over and over again. Being around children of this age requires energy and attention because our little investigators can get into trouble quickly. However, being exposed to toddlers has the inevitable result of reminding the adult of what is wonderful and exciting in life.

A SECOND LOOK

It's hard to believe that it was 18 years ago that I undertook the project of writing this book. What's different eighteen years later? Toddlers aren't different, that's for sure! They are still the wonderful, busy, "scientists" who are endlessly experimenting and discovering how the world works. And the same techniques for working with them that were successful 18 years ago still work now. The main thing that has changed is our knowledge base. There has been a huge growth in the number of programs that serve toddlers. I have enjoyed keeping in touch with people when speaking at conferences, presenting and attending workshops, visiting countless child care programs and writing a column for *Child Care Information Exchange* magazine called "Caring for the Little Ones." Many parents and child care providers have generously shared insights and ideas with me, which I am passing on to you.

PURPOSE

My motivation for writing this book originated with the requests for help from adults who work with toddlers in group child care situations. As I presented my ideas to various groups of people, I learned that it was not just child care center caregivers who were interested in activities for toddlers. I found equal interest from family child care providers, play group supervisors, in-home child care providers, and parents and grandparents who are trying to provide toddlers and twos with a stimulating environment in which to grow and learn. So, although at times this book may address specific situations of toddlers in group care, it is really written for anyone who is looking for ideas and activities that do not merely "occupy" a toddler, but also stimulate the child's natural curiosity and development of intelligence.

WHAT IS A TODDLER?

When I talk about "toddlers" in this book, I am referring to children roughly between the ages of 12 months and about 3 years of age. People have asked me to describe the difference between a toddler and a two-year-old, so I have added Chapter 1, "What is a Toddler? What is a Two-Year-Old?", in which I describe what is happening with this age developmentally. The infant of 12 or 13 months who is just learning to "toddle" is very different from the competent child of 36 months. The learning and development that takes place in this 24-month span of time is truly phenomenal. One of the most exciting things about working with toddlers and two-year-olds is that they seem to be changing every day, and indeed they are! Knowing what interests children, what they can and cannot do, and what they are just ready to do will help in planning activities that will enhance children's development and minimize frustration on the part of both adults and children.

WHAT'S THE SECRET?

As I observed many people working with toddlers in different settings, I noticed that successful teachers and parents seemed "tuned in" to the toddlers. They were able to pick up and expand upon what the children do naturally, building upon children's interests rather than constantly restricting and prohibiting them, while at the same time setting consistent and appropriate limits. They were not so much preoccupied with "teaching" children and cramming endless facts into their young heads as they were in sharing in a child's joy of discovery. They encouraged, arbitrated, explained and demonstrated a knack for providing just the right challenge to the young explorers.

ACTION!

The chapters in this book are organized around verbs – *action* words. Toddlers are busy *doing* stuff. The main focus of the book is on activities – as the title promises, *things to do* with this age. In my observations I focused on what toddlers really *do* most of the time. I noticed that there are certain behaviors that toddlers seem to do over and over again, and you can expect these same behaviors in any toddler, anywhere in the world. At times I felt that these actions (sticking fingers in holes, climbing, etc.) seemed almost compulsive – nature seemed to require that they do it. Believing that toddlers are natural learners, I felt that their compulsive behaviors must have some purpose in their overall learning and development. It usually didn't take too much searching to find the learning value in their natural activities. Whenever children develop a new skill or are just about to master it, they are driven to do it over and over again. This self-imposed drill of "emerging skills" is a natural learning style of toddlers. It is usually fairly simple to build activities around the natural activities children are "driven" to do.

BEHAVIORS

Another new chapter added at the beginning is "Behaving." Biting is a behavior discussed at length in this chapter. It seemed necessary. After presenting hundreds of workshops about working with toddlers, the first question I still hear is, "What can we do about biting?" This is such a big issue of concern when we bring toddlers together in groups that it needs a thorough discussion along with the other types of aggression we see in this age. I'm hoping that when the reader reads the content of this book many of the "preventive" measures have been covered – keeping children marvelously occupied.

SOME TRAINING IDEAS

Each chapter ends with a section called "Frequently Asked Questions," except for Chapters 1 and 3. These are questions I have heard again and again in my personal interactions with toddler caregivers. I do not mean to imply that the answers I offer are the only answers to the questions posed. It would be a fun exercise to use these questions for a staff meeting or workshop. Invite participants to brainstorm answers as a group, without first seeing the answers in the book. Then see how their answers compare to the answers in the book, and discuss.

Another interesting exercise would be to create a visual representation of this book, using the children in your program. Over time, take photos, slides or videotapes of children engaged in the activities you offer them from the book and create a scrapbook, slide show or video presentation you can then show to parents and new staff. Along with the visuals, give explanations of how the children are benefitting from the activities. The very act of creating this visual documentation is excellent training, focusing the caregivers who are acting as photographers on how toddlers learn and on their goals with children.

SAFETY

Safety is always a concern when working with very young children. Their physical instability, combined with their exploratory nature and their compulsion to put everything in the mouth, require that toddlers be closely supervised at all times. I have added a safety note whenever a toy or activity could present an obvious potential danger. Toddlers, however, can manage to hurt themselves on just about anything! It is extremely important to "babyproof" your environment, removing common hazards. The Appendix at the end of the book has a list of safety pointers for your indoor and outdoor environments. Most important, however, is good supervision. Maintain an awareness – stay alert to any possible hazard and never leave children unsupervised by an adult.

BRAIN RESEARCH

The recent research in brain development gives credence to what early childhood professionals and sensitive parents have known for a long time: The first three years of life are extremely important in a child's development. Much of the structure of the brain is engineered during those three years. Experience is the key factor in how a child's brain develops – the activities you present to a child and the opportunities you give the child to explore budding interests in a safe, loving, emotionally supportive environment. If a child were to be kept in a blank room with no stimulation, he would not learn. If a child is kept passive in front of a TV set with little interaction with adults, she will not learn as much as the child who is actively involved with play materials and other human beings. While a child can make up for lost time after the age of three and can still learn, it will never be as easy or as much fun. Working with this age, you have a golden opportunity to help a child become a curious, capable individual, eager to continue life-long learning.

A FINAL THOUGHT

I do not intend to suggest that doing all the activities in this book will ensure a child of superior intelligence. However, much of learning takes place between a child's first and third birthdays. If you are looking for ways to make the time you spend with toddlers more pleasant and interesting for *both* you and the children, this book can help. Respect your toddlers – they are wonderful and at an exciting stage of development. Let them be all they can be by knowing how to work with their natural learning drives.

Karen Miller

THINGS TO DO

WITH

TODDLERS AND

TWOS

PART I

—

UNDERSTANDING THE AGE

CHAPTER 1

What is a **T**oddler?
What is a **T**wo-**Y**ear-**O**ld?

*T*he word, toddler, is vague in its usage. Some people outside the field of early childhood education use the term toddler to refer to any child under kindergarten age. Many child care programs define the toddler age from about 18 months to 2-1/2 years old. This book gives the word a much more literal meaning... "one who toddles," or walks with that choppy, stiff-legged gait, from as soon as the child is up and walking, as young as 10 or 11 months, until about the age of two. A two-year-old, more obviously, is a child between 24 and 36 months of age.

Let's take a look at what happens in this two-year time span. It's a progression. Two-year-olds refine and add complexity to the rough, experimental actions of toddlers. Practice makes better...although they are far from perfect. It is an evolving age. Notice their "self-imposed drill." Whatever skills are emerging...and there are so many of them...need to be practiced over and over again as the child gains mastery.

Keep in mind that each child is different and develops at the pace that is just right for him. Avoid comparing children to each other. Instead, admire and support each child as you watch development unfold and new skills emerge in a unique way.

EMOTIONAL ISSUES

TODDLERS

Trust in the reliability of the caring adult(s) in the child's life was established in the infant year. It came about through sensitive, responsive caregiving. The adults who cared for the child learned to read the baby's signals accurately, knowing what all the various grunts and cries meant, and then relieving the child's stress. This taught the baby that the world is a safe place. When the child enters toddlerhood, this feeling of trust needs to be reestablished and tested again and again. Will that adult be there for me, no matter how far I venture out? Much of the "testing" behavior that can so annoy adults is the child's way of making sure the security blanket is still there. Each child needs an adult "anchor" – some person he trusts most of all. This primary caregiver is the one the child goes to when hurt or in need. Eventually the circle of trust can expand to include several individuals.

Independence, a desire to do things by themselves, comes with the new mobility. There can be tremendous resistance to help, or an adult's attempts to limit or control. Design the environment to be safe for the child to explore independently, with just a distant supervising eye of an adult. Establish consistency in daily routines, so the child knows what to expect and can cooperate independently, as though it was his idea.

Separation is a big issue with toddlers. It comes with their new mobility, and their ability to run away from a parent or caregiver. You can almost see the invisible rubber band that keeps them coming back to touch base with the trusted adult. One minute they run away, demanding independence, the next they are back on a lap, cuddling or demanding attention. Adults should always say good-bye when they are leaving, even if it brings a loud protest by the child. Not sneaking out on a child respects the trust that he has developed in the adult.

Security objects make their entrance in the toddler year. The child finds comfort in one stable thing that is with him all the time, such as a blanket or stuffed animal. No matter how much the world around him changes, this thing is constant. Sometimes called "transitional objects," these can be a symbol of home, a piece of parental love and trust that the child can take with him as he bravely faces the world.

Emotional expressions are part of a toddler's basic communication. Facial expressions and intonations come before words. A toddler leaves no doubt about when he is happy, upset or afraid. There's no ambiguity, no hiding of feelings. It's all right out in the open, "on their sleeve." A sensitive adult should name the emotions the child is expressing, understanding that there are no *bad* emotions. All human beings, including toddlers, have a right to a full range of feelings. Giving children appropriate ways to express feelings is the main teaching task of people who work with toddlers and two-year-olds.

TWO-YEAR-OLDS

Power! Two-year-olds are establishing their place in the universe. Their favorite word, "no," was invented for just this purpose! In addition to resisting direction and suggestions from adults, they also enjoy making things happen.

Fears are a partner of power. Because of their language skills and growing ability to imagine, fears can show up in the two's year, as they sort out what is real and what is fantasy. As the child gains more independence, he also does more thinking about what might happen. The monster under the bed is there only when the parent is out of the room. With growing language ability comes more abstract thinking, but a two-year-old is a long way from figuring out how the world works. He needs the reassuring presence of a trusted adult to help interpret the world and what he might be thinking. The wise adult does not discount the child's fears, but is quietly there, taking the child's emotions seriously, helping the child to cope.

Toilet learning, which usually begins between the child's second and third birthday, is really an issue of emotional control, as well as separation, control, cooperation and being willing to leave an activity to go to the bathroom. It is a physical maturation issue too, of course.

Rituals can be very helpful in giving a two-year-old a sense of power and control. Using the same words and actions for various situations helps make the world predictable.

GROSS MOTOR ISSUES

TODDLERS

Mastering different ways to move their bodies is *the* dominant theme of the toddler year. It's as though they are drunk with the power of their new mobility. Indeed, young toddlers seem almost like drunk drivers as they careen through space, bumping into things and falling down. But their drive to master their emerging skill of walking causes them to get right back up again. You have to admire their courage and perseverance! Learning to get from standing to squatting or sitting and back up again without holding onto something is a major task. Up, down, up, down. It's great fun to watch. Each child develops his own system to get from sitting to standing. Toddlers also love exploring all the other ways to move – crawling in different ways (they are expert at this), tiptoeing, running, rolling, jumping, squatting. Games imitating movements are very popular for this reason.

Speed control is an issue. When they first walk they have trouble slowing down, stopping and turning. When in a hurry, a new walker may drop to all fours and go into four-wheel-drive, some of them achieving amazing speed! But it doesn't take them long to learn how to run, again with difficulty putting on the brakes.

Climbing is another compulsion of this age, starting even before they can walk. They need to sling that leg up and over whatever obstacle presents itself and scale the mountain...because it's there! Find good, stable things for them to climb on, and pad the surface of the floor underneath. Also think about the eventuality that they will climb on things not meant for climbing, like bookshelves and other furniture. Stabilize furniture as much as possible so it's not likely a child can pull it over on himself. This is a major reason this age needs such close supervision. Stay nearby so you can redirect them to things that are okay to climb on.

It is a very **accident-prone** age because they have little control of speed and direction, undependable balance, and no concept of their limitations or the consequences of their misjudgements. As you "babyproof" your environment, be conscious of things children can stumble over, such as area rugs, and pad sharp corners of low tables and other furniture.

TWO-YEAR-OLDS

The choppy gait of the toddlers gradually smooths out. Two-year-olds **bend their knees and ankles when they walk,** can slow down, stop, turn on a dime, walk up and down stairs alternating feet, and generally move smoothly and with assurance. They can actually clear the ground when they jump, and they love jumping off of small platforms.

Now that they've got all this new skill, they like doing **"tricks,"** showing off. They love to imitate each other in funny actions. They also like **moving with objects,** throwing things, twirling hoops, walking around with boxes on their feet, using riding toys, feet on the floor, etc.

With all this new skill, they are driven to practice over and over again. Twos are said to be the **most active age** of early childhood. They have to keep moving. Extra outside time is recommended for this age, as well as provisions for vigorous exercise indoors.

FINE MOTOR ISSUES

TODDLERS

It wasn't long ago that they were just discovering their hands floating out there above them and then gained the skill to aim at things and grasp them. About the time children are learning to toddle they are also learning to **use thumbs and fore-fingers** to pick things up, instead of using a "raking" motion with their whole hand. They derive much pleasure in picking up every tiny dust ball and crumb they find. Another reason to babyproof!

Sticking things in holes is a compulsive activity, as they learn to use their fingers independently, so you might as well find lots of acceptable ways for them to do this. See chapter 9.

Rotating their wrists is another new skill. Young toddlers find out they need to do this when they begin to feed themselves with a spoon. With practice, they become better able to adjust objects held in their hand to fit in a certain way, such as when they learn to use shape boxes and simple fit-together toys.

TWO-YEAR-OLDS

The busy hands of a two-year-old can't wait to manipulate and explore every object that comes his way. **Mechanical devices** and things that open and close in different ways hold interest.

Fit-together toys with more pieces are popular and the child might eventually even start to construct things that represent something. Puzzles with several pieces represent a cognitive challenge as well as a fine-motor challenge.

The child proudly practices **dressing skills** on both his own clothes and those of dolls.

While a two-year-old has difficulty **holding a pencil** the "proper way" for writing, scribbling with a crayon and other art materials allows the child to learn about controlling the direction of the mark being made.

COMMUNICATION ISSUES

TODDLERS

The important thing to know is that **understanding comes before speaking.** While a young toddler cannot express himself with words, he understands a lot of what is said to him. Remember that **language is a lot more than just words.** People gain understanding from the context – what is going on – gestures, facial expressions and tone of voice. Toddlers are good at these things! A sensitive caregiver is usually well aware of what a child wants.

The transition from non-verbal to verbal communication is gradual, but exciting. A young toddler starts out with just a few words he can say, and gradually builds this repertoire of single words. You'll often see a toddler point to things and name them. "What's dat?" becomes a favorite phrase. Social words and greetings, like "hi" and "bye" also come early.

Telegraphic speech comes next – two-word combinations and short phrases.

Not being able to express themselves in more complex social situations can be the cause of much of the frustration in toddlers that can lead to tantrums and even biting. The adult should be an "interpreter" for the child, giving words to what he is feeling and trying to say.

It is extremely important to surround the child with meaningful speech, about what he is seeing and doing right now. This **envelope of language** helps the child add words and meaning daily. Although it varies widely, by the time he turns two he can have between 200 and 500 words at his command.

TWO-YEAR-OLDS

Language adds to the **power** of two-year-olds. **No!** is a favorite word, even when they don't mean it. They can even start to argue...for the pure pleasure of it.

Descriptive words are added to the names of objects. Children can describe things as big, fast, soft, etc.

The child also learns to **ask questions,** such as "Wassat?" while pointing to things. And the child is delighted to learn of his power as he causes adults to respond to his questions.

As children string words together, **grammar** gives them structure. They learn the order the words must come in to make sense, and can start to talk about the past and the future.

Whereas a toddler's language is likely to consist mostly of demands and exclamations, a two-year-old can have a **conversation.** Adults should see how many turns they can take with a child, keeping the conversation going. This builds the child's skill and logical reasoning as one thought leads to another.

With greater verbal ability comes better **social skill** as the child learns to negotiate, ask, and prohibit with words instead of actions.

COGNITIVE ISSUES

The term, "cognitive" can be confusing to people. We generally use this term to talk about "thinking skills" – and yet everything involves thinking, including talking and moving. It's about logic – and at the toddler and two's stage, this means cause and effect. One set of actions causes something else to happen. It's also about relationships of size, space and time. Using symbols is also cognitive – the idea that one thing can represent something else for which one must maintain a mental image. There is a cognitive aspect to all activities.

TODDLERS

Power is once again our starting point. A baby learns about **cause and effect.** A cry causes something to happen. Toddlers continue to explore this. Toys and activities that feature cause and effect are real favorites of this age.

Spaces and shapes – what fits into what – is another exploration of toddlerhood. **Object hunger** is a term used in toddlerhood. They endlessly explore objects for both cause and effect and to see what that shape and material does.

Late in the infant year, children develop **object permanence,** the idea that something continues to exist, even though they can't see it. They have to maintain a mental image of the object. They continue to test the principle well through the toddler year, with peek-a-boo and its many variations being a most popular game.

Using **symbols** is another cognitive skill. A child can be comforted by **pictures** of parents when the parent is absent, and they learn to point to pictures and name the thing they represent.

TWO-YEAR-OLDS

Two-year-olds become more complex in their use of symbols, seen especially in their pretend play, using one object to represent something else.

Concepts of time such as the days of the week or telling time are still beyond two-year-olds, but they are developing time words like *now, later, yesterday, tomorrow*. They understand the sequence of events – bath, story, bed – and sometimes reflect that in their play. They are developing the ability to remember and associate events with people.

Twos will also enjoy books with a simple story line, such as *The Three Bears*, reflecting both advancing language skills and cognitive sequencing of events.

SOCIAL ISSUES

TODDLERS

Most of toddlers' social interactions are with adults. However, with experience and a little protective guidance from an adult, there can be friendships among toddlers. They are **very interested in other children.** They like watching each other and playing near each other. You see this interest in their imitation of other children's actions, and even their bumbling attempts to take away a toy. It may be their way of wanting to play with someone. They laugh when others laugh, joining in the social spirit of glee.

TWO-YEAR-OLDS

With the greater language skills of two-year-olds, you see more and more **social interactions with peers.** They very slowly learn the advantages of sharing and taking turns and the fun of playing with something together. Funny noises, silliness, funny faces will draw giggles. While they are still egocentric, seeing the world and situations from their own point of view, their circle is broadening and they are beginning to think of the other child. Their dramatic play may begin to involve other children, especially if an adult plays along.

KEEPING TRACK

Every child is unique – a wonder unto himself. Keep a record of the child's development to remind you of where he is coming from and help you plan and modify activities. There are many effective ways to do this.

- **Journal.** Jot down and date ongoing notes of your observations of the child. Include things such as the emergence of new skills, how the child reacted to new materials or activities, social developments, illnesses, separation difficulties and resolutions, language developments, etc.

- **Portfolio**. A file folder could contain journal notes described above, art work, photos, and tape recordings of the child's language.

- **Scrapbook.** Like the portfolio, it is a little more portable and easier to save.

- **Photo Album.** Use a camera in a systematic way, such as photographing the child doing something new once a month, to document growth, coordination, interests and social life. Add descriptive written comments.

- **Videos.** Videotape the child for a few minutes once a month. Try to catch him practicing some new skill. You'll end up with a living baby book.

CHAPTER 2

BEHAVING

*T*he director of the child care center, also the mother of a two-year-old, was driving home with her child. "Amanda," she said, "you had a really rough day today. You pulled hair. You splashed water out of the water table on purpose. You even bit Robert." Amanda listened with a worried look on her face. Suddenly she brightened and said, "But I didn't spit!"

This chapter could have been titled: "Hitting, Biting, Pulling, Screaming." Dealing with difficult behaviors is one of the more challenging things about working with toddlers and two-year-olds. Instead, the chosen title of this chapter, "Behaving," is meant to be neutral…a way of helping the reader observe that children are simply "acting" or "behaving" in ways to get their needs met. Often, in fact, the behavior they choose is counterproductive. They draw attention to themselves, make things happen, force the issue, to try to gain some power in a situation, but they can end up annoying people and even hurting their peers and adult friends.

Our goal is to go back to the neutral meaning of the word "behave," as in "act," and help children figure out how to meet their needs in ways that are okay with everybody. We have to remember that they are just learning how to do this. To help them, the adult needs to offer them new strategies to try, *and give them repeated practice to make the behavior automatic* when new situations come up. So, the adult must do a lot of talking, explaining, demonstrating, supporting, *coaching*.

It's usually pretty easy to figure out what is going on – what the child's emotions are and what she is trying to accomplish. What's wonderful about this age is that they are "people without the shell." The layers of protection have not been added yet. They haven't learned to hide their emotions. They wear their emotions right out there for everyone to see. You can help them come to terms with their feelings.

PREVENTIVE TECHNIQUES

Just by doing certain things, you can prevent conflict from arising and give children more successful social experiences.

ANTICIPATE

"Head them off at the pass." "Catch it on the build." Experienced caregivers list this first when talking about how to help children in discipline situations. You can usually feel the tension building, or sense a difficult situation developing and move in to suggest a different solution. Experience will teach you when, and what circumstances are likely to lead to problems. Children are more likely to be aggressive when they are hungry or tired. A new toy is difficult to share, and you might decide to have some of the children outside with another adult when the toy is brought out. You'll know when play is getting too wild and you need to calm children down and divert them into another activity.

STAY CLOSE

Get close. It only makes sense that if you are near the children you can sense trouble building and intervene before trouble erupts. But you can also gently lead children into play you know is less likely to cause tension, and reinforce good behavior. Your very presence can serve as a reminder to older children who have learned to get along but can find it diffi-cult to remember. You can interpret children to each other, helping them to hear what the other is trying to say, and to be heard and understood themselves.

CHOOSE YOUR BATTLES

Toddlers need to win some of their battles. Does it really mat-ter that he wants the red chair, not the yellow one? If you can be accommodating some of the time, the child will feel less pressured to assert her power in all situations. Decide which things you will be firm on and stick to them. If children sense they will *never* be allowed to climb onto the table top, even-tually they will stop pushing this limit.

PLAN THE ENVIRONMENT

We know that toddlers are more apt to lash out if they are crowded. So we arrange the environment to allow children to spread out in their activities. We know that they fight over toys, so we arrange to have enough things for them to play with, and duplicates of popular toys. We know that like everybody, they get tense if there is nothing but hard furni-ture and surfaces around, so we arrange to have soft, cozy places. We know that like anyone, they get tired of being with a large group all the time, so we arrange for nooks and cran-nies so they can be off by themselves from time to time.

BALANCE ACTIVITIES

Create a balance of active play and quiet play. Too much of

either one can create tension. Children can get physically tired from too much active play, or too long a walk. But requiring them to sit still too long, listening to stories, or engaging in quiet table play can be stressful too. Since the right balance may be different for each child, plan to have choices of both active and quiet play both outside and inside. Usually children will choose what they need, but sometimes you might need to make the suggestion and change what they are doing.

HAVE A CONSISTENT ROUTINE

You will avoid a lot of battles if you have a consistent daily routine. Do the same thing in the same way every day. This gives children a sense of security – that they know how things happen here. You won't have to tell them what to do and how to do it all the time, and get their resistance. They will coop-erate automatically, demonstrating their power and skill in a situation, for instance always going to put on coats to go out-side immediately after snack if you always go outside then.

REDUCE TENSION

There are many things that can reduce the level of tension and can help children relax a little:

- Sensory play with materials like water, sand, play dough
- Soft things like cushions and stuffed animals
- One-on-one time with an adult
- Reading calming books
- Calm music
- Outdoor play to let children run off excess energy

GIVE INDIVIDUAL ATTENTION

Sometimes children's "acting out" behavior is simply their way of saying, "Pay attention to me!!!" So, make sure that you carve out some one-on-one time with each child each day, starting with a warm greeting in the morning. It can be as little as a conversation about what they did last night, or more concentrated, such as an extended play time, with the adult following the child's lead, letting the child decide what to play with and how to proceed with the materials. You're giving the child attention and power.

BUILD ON SUCCESS

Notice out loud when children are getting along well, but do so in a subtle way. "I love to watch you two play together. You're having so much fun sharing that truck." "Good job, Jenny. You told Cindy she could have it in a minute and that helped her wait." In this way you are helping children feel competent, and you reinforce social skills they are learning.

BUILD LANGUAGE SKILLS

Most difficult behavior comes from the toddler's inability to negotiate with words. With this age it isn't enough to tell a child to "use words." She needs you to supply the words. Give her phrases to parrot. "Caitlin, say, 'I have this now.'" "Wyatt, tell him, 'I don't like that!'" "Brittany, say, 'You can have this in a minute, when I'm through.'" Then help her be heard and understood. "Nick, did you hear what Brittany said? She said you could have it in a minute." Then help Nick find something else to do.

BE A ROLE MODEL

Toddlers are great imitators. Talk to them in a kind, gentle way, and also be very conscious of how you interact with other adults when a child is around. Express your reactions too. "It hurts my feelings when you shout at me. Can you say it like this? 'Miss Judy, I want you to read the other book now.'" "Thank you…that feels much better to me." And be aware that every time you are dealing with a difficult child or intervening in a difficult situation the other children are all

ears, learning from everything you say and do. You are building skills when you handle other children firmly, but with
respect.

DEALING WITH THE SITUATION AT HAND

In spite of everything you do to prevent it, some conflict
between children is inevitable. If you intervene quickly and
well, the children can actually learn some skills to use on their
own at a later time.

DISTRACT

Young toddlers, especially, are easy to distract when they des-
perately want what the child next to them is playing with.
Offer them something different, and make it even more
appealing by playing with it yourself a little, and often the
child will go along with your idea.

REDIRECT

If a child is doing something not allowed, try to find the clos-
est possible thing for her to do that is okay. "It's not okay to
throw sand because it could get in someone's eyes and that
hurts. But here's a whole bunch of balls that are okay to
throw." "It's not okay to climb on the bookshelf. Let's go over
here to the climber and you can show me how you can
climb." "Pulling hair hurts, Lily. Here's a doll with long hair
you can pull." Give children many possible ways to do
acceptably what they have to do. This book is full of possible
redirection activities.

IGNORE

If nobody is getting hurt or is in danger of being hurt, sometimes it's best to ignore it and let the children work it out
themselves. This is the hardest thing for an adult to do! With

our adult sense of fairness, it's hard to see one child take advantage of another, such as when they grab a toy away. But it usually works itself out and children gain experience at being on "both ends of the stick." They need a certain amount of this before they can learn empathy – to put themselves in someone else's shoes. If you sense that one child is always the victim, you can work to build that child's skills in expressing herself.

INTERVENE, STOP, SEPARATE...WITH LANGUAGE

Naturally, there are times when you'll simply have to step in and take over, especially if there is danger of anyone getting hurt. Always surround your actions with language, and treat children with respect, even when they are misbehaving. Acknowledge what they are feeling. "I know you are angry because you don't want to go inside now, Hannah, but it's not okay to throw things and hurt people. We'll come outside again this afternoon." "Shawn, you seem to have trouble playing with Tomas today. Come over here and play with Erin and me for awhile." "Lisa, hurting people is not okay. I know he took your book. Next time tell him, 'I have this now.' But now, I want you to play over here at the play dough table."

PRACTICE POSITIVE BEHAVIORS

To learn something, children need many opportunities to practice. Being in a social group with other children will automatically provide this. You can plan situations where children can reinforce their new skills and then notice and congratulate them for handling it well. See the "Pro-Social Play" section in chapter 15 about friendship for many ways to give children successful experiences with give and take. The idea is to think of many ways children can enjoy playing together. This helps the child feel capable. Learning to share and taking turns are discussed at greater length in that chapter as well.

"Floor Time"

Dr. Stanley Greenspan describes a play method he calls "Floor Time" in his book *The Essential Partnership* (Viking, 1989). This is when you get down on the floor and play with a child, one-on-one, and follow the child's lead. You start by doing what the child is doing – "parallel playing" with the child. Then you expand a little – add a new idea – and see if the child responds. You can also build on ideas the child adds, forming "circles" of communication through your play. The important thing is to allow the child to be the leader. You set the stage – provide play materials and time, but allow the child to be the director of the play, whether you're in the sandbox digging, playing with trucks and blocks, or involved in pretend play. This type of play with an adult is good for all children. It gives them a sense of power and worth, and there's no better way to build a relationship with a child than by playing with him.

When a child has had a difficult time and you have had to impose limits and intervene, then if it is at all possible, settle down as quickly as possible with that child for some "Floor Time" play. Stanley Greenspan even suggests that parents and caregivers double the amount of "Floor Time" play you would normally give a child after a difficult situation. What you are doing is re-establishing a relationship with the child and in a sense, letting the child vent a little frustration in acceptable ways, while getting your positive attention.

PRACTICES TO AVOID

- Do not use any kind of physical punishment, especially shaking. It can be very dangerous, and you are only being a role model for violence.
- Do not wash out the mouth with soap. It's ineffective, and a form of physical punishment that simply gives kids the

example of doing bad things to someone else.

- Do not bite them back. It teaches that it's okay to hurt someone if you're bigger than they are.
- Do not humiliate a child by calling attention to a misdeed in front of others, or standing her in the corner. Humiliation breeds resentment and will ruin your relationship with the child.
- Do not label a time-out chair. It's humiliating, and time out doesn't work with this age group.
- Do not make children apologize, give a kiss and make up, etc. They don't mean it and will only learn to use that behavior to manipulate.
- Do not send the child to the director's office. The child learns that you can't handle her, and it's usually fun in the director's office anyway, and the child gets extra attention.
- Do not compare children to each other or hold someone up for a good example. You can say, "I like the way Sarah is sitting still..." but don't say, "Why can't you be nice like Sarah?" That only breeds resentment.
- Do not tell a child she is acting like a baby or threaten to send her to the baby room.
- Do not use food as rewards or punishments. It puts undue value on food and could lead to eating disorders later.
- Do not use stickers, candy, names on the board, star charts, etc. for rewards. Children act only for the reward and won't act without it. You'll have to keep increasing the reward.
- Do not tell children to "be good." It's way too vague. One can make a mistake and still be a "good" person.
- Do not say, "If you two can't play nicely with that toy I'm going to put it away." They never learn how to negotiate that way.

Some of these "bad practices" might put a stop to the immediate behavior, but may even strengthen the undesirable behavior in the long run. You are just *punishing* and not *teaching* in these situations.

BE AWARE OF DIFFERENT TEMPERAMENTS

You already do this. You know that you need to give certain
children more slack than others. Some children are more
easygoing, others blow up at the least aggravation. It's important to realize that there are no "bad" temperaments. A child's
emotional make-up is something she is born with. But you
can help a child learn to cope and you can learn to work well
with all temperaments. There are three basic temperaments:

- **Slow to warm up, fearful, shy, sensitive** are words that
  describe one basic temperament. This is the child who
  hangs back and watches other children a long time before
  joining in play. The child might be easily frightened or
  overwhelmed. She really needs the adult "anchor," a trusted adult to stay right with her and be accessible. Rather
  than force a child to participate, present activities and let
  her approach on her own terms. Be there for the child, but
  don't do too much for her.

- **Flexible, easygoing, cooperative, "sunny"** is another temperament type. The majority of children fall into this category. The child is generally in a good mood, cooperative,
  and eager to do everything you offer. The difficulty with
  this temperament is that it can be easy for the adult to
  ignore this child, distracted with the needs of other children who are more demanding. These children need adult
  attention just as much, and even though they may be more
  willing to wait, they greatly benefit from your interest and
  play.

- **Feisty, difficult, "short fuse," active, irritable** can describe
  another temperament. Note that these are mostly negative
  adjectives. Adults sometimes have to work a little harder at
  "liking" these children because they can cause more problems and spoil adult plans. While a flexible child might
  issue a mild protest when a toy is taken away, a feisty one
  can launch into a full-blown tantrum or aggressive behav-

ior. Remember, this is not a "bad" temperament...it is just the way the child is. You naturally stay more aware of her and are wise to anticipate what might be stressful. She will need more of a warning for transitions in the routine, for example. The feisty child can also be delightful in her quick thinking and mischievousness. So build on the positives and give the child many ways to express herself in fun and joyful ways.

SOME SPECIFIC SITUATIONS

TANTRUMS

When a child throws herself on the floor in a fit of kicking and screaming, it is distressing to everyone around. This child is clearly out of control...saying, in effect, "This is too much, too much, I cannot deal with it. Help me!" She needs an empathetic response, and the sense that the adult is strong and in control so she can feel safe. It helps to know the difference between a tantrum that comes from pure, utter frustration, and one that is used to manipulate. As you get to know the child well, you may be able to anticipate what will lead to a tantrum and avoid getting her into that position.

- Don't let the tantrum "work." The child must not get her way because of this behavior, or, of course, she will use it again and again when things aren't going her way.
- Sympathize, but stay firm. "Yes, I know. It's hard to wait for your turn. But you will learn, and I am here to help you."
- Let the tantrum play itself out. Make the child comfortable. You can't force her to stop because once started, often she can't stop until the tension is blown off. "You can be over here until you calm down. We'll be over there. Come and join us when you are ready." Give the child a pat of reassurance.
- Sometimes offering a screaming child a glass of water

helps her calm down and take a breath, offering her a
graceful way out.
• When the tantrum plays itself out, welcome the child back
  to the group and try to help her solve her problem. "Phew!
  That was scary for you and it hurt our ears. Let's talk about
  what you can do next time you want..." You could give
  the child some phrases to parrot, or act out a situation in
  pretend play.

HITTING, SCRATCHING, PUSHING, POKING... HURTING

"It's not okay to hurt people," is the message you want to get
across. You intervene quickly when a child hurts another, or
you sense it is about to happen.

• Step in and interrupt the action.
• Point out that the other child is crying because it hurts.
• Say, "I don't want you to hurt Jamie. That's not okay."
• Help the victim child say something like, "I don't like
  that!"
• Help the aggressor come up with words to express herself
  to the other child. But do not force her to say she's sorry.
• You might invite the aggressor to find a way to comfort the
  victim.
• If necessary, separate the children and involve them in
  totally different activities.

HAIR PULLING

It's often the younger toddlers who engage in hair pulling.
What starts out as exploration turns into a cause-and-effect
toy. They may like the feel of the hair in their hands and discover by accident that it causes a scream. It's important to dis-
tinguish between hair pulling that is done out of exploration
or investigation, and that which is done out of aggression. For
the exploring child, it can help to offer the child a doll with
long hair she can pull instead. You might also try letting the

child play with a wig attached to a foam head wig holder. "It hurts Tilly when you pull her hair. I don't want you to hurt our friends. But you can pull this doll's hair all you want to." With the other child's permission and you right there, you can also show the child how to feel hair gently. Put your hand over the child's and first let her feel her own hair, then your hair, then the other child's hair gently, and talk about how the hair feels.

When the child pulls hair for aggression, you treat it the same way you would any other hurting behavior.

BITING

"What do you do about biting?" This question has come up at virtually every conference involving toddler care. It is a common problem facing people who provide group care for toddlers. Unfortunately, there is no simple solution. A lot depends on the age of the child and the situation that led to the biting.

WHY DO TODDLERS BITE?

Not *all* toddlers bite other children. Children who never bite at home will use this behavior when in the presence of other children, such as group child care, a play date with another toddler friend or a birthday party. Sometimes a toddler classroom will go for months and months without a biting incident and then suddenly there's a "rash" of biting. There are a number of things that might lead to biting. You start from the reason and then try to give the child a more acceptable way of getting her needs met.

Teething

Toddlers are cutting teeth and it hurts. Chewing on something relieves the itch and makes it feel better. Since there are so many other things to chew on, teething is probably not the reason toddlers bite other children.

Have things that are okay to bite. Keep a bowl of carrot sticks around. Tell a child, "If you need to bite something, tell me, and I'll get you a carrot stick." You could also keep small, dish washing size sponges in plastic zip close bags in the refrigerator for this purpose. No need to take them out of the bag. Let the child chew on these cold sponge-filled bags when there seems to be teething pain. Or, put clean wash cloths, which were wet and wrung out, in the freezer. This requires that you stay alert and perceptive of children's teething distress.

Sensory Exploration

This is a very "oral" stage of development. They chew on *everything*, not just their fellow man. Both the sense of taste and the sense of touch are rewarded through biting. Sometimes children bite a child who is new to the group as a way to find out more about them.

Give children plenty of opportunities to release tension through tactile experiences. Water play is especially soothing. Play dough also allows children to squeeze out tensions. As for the new child, encourage children to come over to her and see her and touch her while you are right there (not all at once, of course). It may help.

Cause and Effect

It's almost like their interest in something like a jack-in-the-box toy. Young toddlers are constantly studying cause and effect and are amazed to find out that they have the *power* to make something happen. With biting, an action produces a predictable response – and what a response! There's a magnificent noise. Everything in the room comes to a stop. The adult in the room is sure to appear instantly. You are likely to get picked up.

There are lots of ways you can allow children to cause legitimate effects on their environment. Of course, if you perceive the effect they're after is to get your attention, that's another matter. The obvious and simplest answer is to give them more attention. Look at children. Use their names. Smile. Pick them up and waltz with them for no apparent reason *before* they bite.

Mimicking

This may be why after a long "biteless" period, you suddenly have a bunch of biters! Children learn behaviors from other children, just like cup banging, waving bye-bye, etc.

The only thing you can do here is give a strong message that this behavior is not approved, and give them lots of positive behaviors to imitate instead, like using language.

Frustration

This is the main reason toddlers bite. Self-assertion. Instant power! It's a way to express frustration when they don't yet have the language skills to do so. Biting, a child learns, is the quickest and most efficient way to register a protest.

First, take a good critical look at your program and try to cut down on frustration to toddlers. Avoid crowding children. Stay within licensing standards for square footage per child, and make sure your room arrangement isn't forcing children all into one area. Keep them happily occupied with interesting activities and they are less likely to bite.

Work diligently and daily on building children's verbal communication skills – both in giving messages and receiving messages. "Johnny, say 'Stop – don't hit me!'" "Tell her with words instead of screams, Jenny. Say, 'I'm using this now.'" "Jason, do you hear Jenny? She said 'Mine.' That means she's using that now. You can have it when she's through. Here's another puzzle you can use."

"Head them off at the pass." If you see frustration building in a child – grabbing toys or fighting with other children, screaming, whining, tantrums, etc. – redirect the child. Intervene, and get her involved in something else.

WHAT DO YOU DO WHEN BITING OCCURS?

Sometimes classroom conditions can be just fine and children will still bite. It just happens too fast for effective intervention. The first thing you have to do, of course, is attend to the victim. Put ice on the area immediately. If there is a break in the skin, the area must be thoroughly cleaned immediately. Depending on the severity, it may need attention from a physician.

Give a strong message of disapproval. Show that it hurts the other child.

The trouble is, toddlers don't have a sense of the "realness" of other people. They must *learn* empathy. Bring the biter face to face with the victim. Your voice should be angry without yelling. Say to the biter something like: "Biting hurts! Lisa is crying because you hurt her very much! Look at her eyes, there are tears coming out. It's not okay to bite!" Research has shown that it's important to give a strong, empathetic, emotional response. Look angry, talk angry, no sweet-talk double messages. Emphasize how it hurts the victim.

Help the victim express herself.

If you can, get the victim to say, "It hurts. I don't want you to bite me!"

Involve the biter in comforting the victim.

Model an empathetic response to the victim. Show concern

for the hurt. Let the biter see you hug the victim and say you are sorry that happened to her. Say out loud, "Let's see what we can do to make the hurt go away." Don't force the biter to say she's sorry. That only breeds insincerity. But you can invite the biter to get a cold cloth to put on the bruised area, or find the victim's special security toy to bring to her to make her feel better. Just be careful that the biter isn't enjoying the extra attention that she is getting as "the comforting one" so that she bites again in order to play the role. If you sense that is what is going on, it is a clear message that the biter needs more positive attention from you in non-aggressive situations.

Ease the re-entry.

Involve the child in something totally different from what she was doing before – something soothing like play dough. You need to get this child back into a positive mode as quickly as possible. When you have a few minutes, involve the biter in some extra "Floor Time" (see above), without stating or implying it is because she bit someone earlier. You need to re-establish a positive relationship with this child.

WHAT DO YOU DO ABOUT THE CHRONIC BITER?

Involve the other children in teaching the biter.

You or a puppet could say something like, "We have a problem in this class. Melissa gets mad and sometimes she forgets that it's not okay to bite people. So, when you think Melissa is going to bite, say, 'NO BITING!'" The biter can be involved in this discussion. Give the message that you are trying to help the biter be a good friend who is fun to play with. Let the children (including the biter) practice saying, "No biting!" Congratulate their efforts, especially when successful. Surprisingly, this has actually stopped some biters in their tracks. It seems to interrupt the impulse.

Give the chronic biter her own special teething toy.

This has nothing to do with teething, but more to do with special attention. Get a new, attractive teething toy. Tell the child, "This is just for you. It is special, because it will help you remember not to bite people. It's easy! Whenever you want to bite someone, bite this instead!" Then attach the teether to the child's clothing with a short strap. Rehearse the child and give positive feedback. "Okay…pretend you want to bite. What do you do? That's right…bite the toy! Good job! Do it again. Good!" Clap your hands. Several times during the day, when you feel even a little bit of tension rising in the biter, coach the child to bite the teether and clap when she does it. Another reason this is a successful intervention might be that the toy is a physical reminder that the child has with her at all times. It could be like Dumbo's magic feather – giving the child confidence that she can deal with a situation.

Take notes, study the situation, ask for help.

When you have a lot of biting in the room, or one child is biting a lot, it is a signal that something is not right. Try to be analytical. Start by taking notes about when the child bites and what led up to it. Also make a note of what you did afterwards, and how the child responded. Ask your director or program supervisor, or another trusted friend who knows about children if you work in family child care, to observe your program at the time of day when biting is most likely to occur. Maybe they will pick up on something you missed. The parent of the biter might be able to help in this way as well, although his or her presence is likely to change the situation for the biter. Try different strategies. Keep everyone informed.

Work with the parents.

At the top of the list of caregivers' most unpleasant tasks is notifying a parent when his or her child has been bitten.

Parents are often angry – outraged that you could let this happen. They often want to know which child did the biting, if their child cannot tell them. Giving the name is rarely a good idea. It is counterproductive, and could lead to a confrontation between parents. They often demand that the biter be disenrolled from the program, which is rarely the right solution to the problem. Instead, tell them what you are doing to deal with the situation and lessen the chances of a recurrence. Point out also, that it might be their child who bites another time.

It can be just as distressing to tell the parent of the biter what happened. The parents of the biter may be on the defensive, thinking you are blaming them, and may fear losing child care. They may ask you what you are doing to cause the child to want to bite someone. Parents often tell staff to bite the child back. Although this may convey the message that biting causes pain, it is a remedy that absolutely should be prohibited. The real message that it gives is that it's okay for adults to hurt people but not for children.

The stress of this all may be lessened if parents are forewarned. Not that you *expect* biting, but let them know that it is not an uncommon behavior. You should talk about this in your enrollment interview with the parents, or when the child is promoted into your room from the infant program. Let parents know that although this is a "normal" behavior of toddlers in groups, not an indication that the child is seriously disturbed, you take it very seriously and do all you can to prevent it. Describe some of the preventive things you do. And describe what will happen if a child bites.

The real key to prevent biting in your program is to keep children busy and happy, touch and hug a lot, cut down on toddler frustration, and give children a lot of individual attention. Do what you can to develop empathy in toddlers by describing *feelings* of other children…all sorts of feelings. Organize with fellow staff so one person's function for a given period is to handle "custodial" matters, diapering, etc., leaving the other staff free to be the "play person," directly involved with the children. Reinforce positive behaviors: "You wanted that doll, Jenny, but you waited for Jason to finish. Good job!" "Good talking, Joe! You used words to tell her what you want."

A FEW MORE THOUGHTS

When you are handling a difficult situation, it can help to pretend you are being observed – it makes you behave in the most professional manner possible. So mentally put a respected college professor, one of the parents, or someone else you respect, like television's Mister Rogers, in the room with you. How would you want them to see you responding to this child?

Do some "positive imaging" for a difficult child. Imagine that you have worked successfully with the child and she is already behaving in exactly the way you would want. How would you greet the child? How would you interact during play times when all is going well? How would you support the child when a conflict arises? Sometimes acting "as if" actually helps the child live up to that image.

A home visit can help when you've had a difficult time with a child. You may gain insights into her behavior. Be sure to tell parents that you are not visiting to "check them out" or inspect their home in any way, or to find a way to blame them. Instead, you are establishing a friendship and familiarity that may make it easier to collaborate. The child may see you more as a special friend and be easier to reach.

Finally, be careful not to blame the child. It's easy to do! When a child repeatedly spoils your plans, hurts other children, embarrasses you in front of colleagues and parents and makes you feel ineffective, it is easy to feel angry at that child.

Remember that young children do not make plans and lay traps. They just act and react. Misbehavior is a cry for help. When a child chronically misbehaves, we correctly fear for her future if effective intervention is not made. But in early childhood, there is still time to help. The child is still malleable. We can still make a difference. Don't be discouraged when a child resorts to previous behavior. Progress will be sporadic. As with all types of learning, she will make mistakes along the way. Help her build on successes.

FREQUENTLY ASKED QUESTIONS

What if the parents have a different discipline style from yours?

It can be discouraging when a parent seems unconcerned and says, "Just slap her." Work to build rapport with the parent. The parent must feel liked and respected before he or she can hear what you are saying and try new things. Empathize. It's hard to be a parent. Focus on your mutual concern for the child. Offer them information in the form of article reprints and books. See them as collaborators as you figure out how to help their child learn acceptable behavior. Phrase everything in an experimental way. Let's try this and see what happens. If all this fails, comfort yourself by knowing that you are giving the child a good example while she is with you and she can still learn.

What if the two parents are inconsistent in discipline, or grandparents are?

Although consistency is best, nobody is absolutely consistent with someone else. Children learn to act in different ways in different settings, and what they can get away with in each. Build on the positives. If a child learns effective ways to interact, that will eventually become her preferred way of behaving.

Nothing we try works. The child seems to be getting worse and worse.

If you find yourself with a really challenging child, become a good detective. Find out as much as you can about the child. Start by studying the enrollment forms. Work with the parents in a collaborative way. Take good notes – keep a journal. It can help you notice patterns of behavior, and it also documents what you have tried. Finally, recognize when you are in over your head, and call in some extra help. Ask other colleagues to observe. Or recommend that the family consult with their pediatrician and inquire about resources for children and families in the community. Important – ask to be part of the circle that supports that child, so you can all work together.

Would you ever disenroll a child because of behavior problems?

Parents don't have the option of "disenrolling" the child from the family. As a good supportive family would do, you should try, and try some more, to help the child learn different behaviors, calling in help if it is needed. It is the most important learning that the child can have at this stage of development. On very rare occasions, when you feel certain that your program is not a good place for the child at this time, you might either recommend a more therapeutic program in your area, or offer the child a "sabbatical" and invite her to return after a month or two away.

CHAPTER 3

Tricks of the Trade — Strategies for Teaching Toddlers and Two-Year-Olds in Groups

*T*oddlers aren't preschoolers. This statement becomes more obvious when people try to get toddlers to do something like raise their hands if they know the answer, line up, get in a circle, wait their turn, sit still and listen, etc. They resist directions and commands, but they want to do what everyone else is doing. They are fearful of strange-looking characters, but they are attracted to whatever is new.

The techniques in this chapter have been picked up from skillful parents and caregivers who are "tuned in" to toddlers and two-year-olds. Instead of trying to make children do things that are difficult or impossible for them, these adults notice what they do naturally and use that to attract and keep their attention.

Surprise Them

One of a two year old's favorite words is "surprise." Saying "I have a surprise for you" is a sure way to get their attention. One caregiver brings in a "surprise" each day in a paper grocery sack. It is usually a common household item like rubber gloves or a hand mixer for children to talk about and examine. But because it is a "surprise" it takes on new interest.

Flop and Do

You try to gather children for a story or some group activity. You succeed in getting two or three over to where you want them. By the time you bring the others over, the first ones are up and gone already.

Often, it seems, the most effective way to introduce a new activity to toddlers is to simply "flop down" and start doing it. No words of introduction or invitation are usually necessary. Children will simply gravitate over to you. They are enticed by your activity and interest rather than compelled by some adult command. This responds to their growing need to make their own decisions. The children who are developmentally ready and interested in what you're doing will be with you.

Likewise, if you want to generate interest in a toy, just start playing with it yourself. This is a way to re-interest children in toys that have been around for a while.

Make It New

No matter how many toys are available, it's always the new one that toddlers want to play with. The newly introduced toy can even be of far less play value or be less attractive than the other toys and still attract attention. You can turn this phenomenon to your advantage. It's a good idea to "rotate" toys, putting some away for several weeks or more. When you bring them out again they will be like new toys in their appeal to toddlers.

Divide and Conquer

If all the children rush over and crowd into one space wanting to do the same thing at the same time, get something going in a different space to draw some of them off. For instance, if all the children crowd into the sandbox when you go outside, announce that you're bringing out the collection of balls, and the riding toys as well, for anyone interested. You might have to announce, "There are too many people in this space right now. I'll come and get you to play here a little later when there is more room."

Give Power

Power is a real theme for toddlers and two-year-olds. They seem to resist every suggestion you make. "No" is a favorite word. They are finding out that they have a say in the way things happen, and are constantly testing this.

Naturally, there are many times when a young child must do what the adult wishes whether he wants to or not – like putting on boots in wet weather or putting away toys at a certain time. But they will be more cooperative if they have plenty of other times to make choices for themselves. What *can* toddlers do for themselves and what real decisions can you engineer for them? Here are some starting ideas for you:

- Ask children's advice and opinions when you're prepared to go with their choices. "Do you think we ought to go outside now or shall we wait till after snack?" "Which CD shall I put on for nap time?" "Shall we put out the clay or the play dough on that table?" "Do you feel like playing with water today?" "Shall we have snack outside or inside today?" "Do you want yellow or blue?"

- When a child produces a work of art let him decide where to hang it. Simply put a piece of tape on it and let the child put it up. (You can take it down to send home after a day or two.)

- Instead of sitting everyone down at the table at the same time for an art project, simply announce, "I've got some paint and sponges and paper over at the art table for anyone who wants to paint. Susie will be over there to help

you if you decide to do that. It will be there all morning."
As the morning progresses Susie can invite individuals to
paint when space becomes available, but children should
be allowed to decline.

- "Would you like orange slices or apple slices for snack? Or
  both?" (Hint: usually, when you offer toddlers a choice,
  they will choose the last thing you mentioned.)

- With self-help routines, children can learn to wash their
  own hands, take off and put on their own socks and shoes,
  take care of most of their own toilet routines, get a drink,
  hang up their coats, wash their faces, etc. Encourage parents to dress their children in clothing that is easy to put on
  and take off themselves.

- Children enjoy helping with basic routines. Setting the
  table, handing out napkins, clearing dishes, setting out
  mats at nap time, putting away toys, turning off lights,
  handing out paper and art supplies, washing brushes, etc.,
  are all things children can help with. Sure, it takes a little
  longer. Justify the time by considering this part of your
  basic curriculum.

- Notice children's spontaneous play activities and expand
  on them. When you hear some spontaneous singing, join
  in. Repeat children's nonsense syllable chants. When someone starts dancing to music get others to do it, too.

- Allow children not to participate – don't feel they have to
  function as a group all the time. Work it out with other
  staff, as to who will supervise a special project and who
  will keep an eye on the rest of the group.

Change the Pace

A wise caregiver knows when to bring out something new or
make something new happen. It is half an hour into the free

play time. Small skirmishes begin, there is a rise in the noise level and more "squawking." Time to put away the play dough and open up the cornmeal table. It gives children a new start. Or you might flop down with a box of special books or bring out your pet puppet, or start a follow the leader game that gets children active. This kind of change of activity can extend the time children play peacefully and enjoy themselves.

Organize for Success

Toddlers carry things around the room, dump containers full of toys and generally mess the place up quickly. It is true that toddlers like to carry things around. It often doesn't matter what, just so there is something in their hands. And dumping...well, that's part of their compulsion of emptying and filling containers. These toddler characteristics can be very frustrating to caregivers who have set up "interest centers" and like to keep a neat, orderly room. This is definitely one area where we must not allow adult needs or preferences to overshadow children's needs. This is not to say you must let children randomly tear the place apart, either.

Organize and simplify your environment. Get a sturdy container for each toy, put a picture label on it, and designate a special place for each toy to be put away with another matching picture. Frequent pleasant reminders will often get matter-of-fact cooperation. "Put the book back on the shelf, Kevin." You will probably learn to limit the number of toys with lots of pieces that you have out for children at any one time. If you set these out on a table top rather than just leaving them on a low shelf, children will be more likely to sit down and play with them in a systematic way.

Finally, don't let the mess accumulate all day until it is overwhelming. Designate several cleanup times during the day – before snack, before you go outside, before lunch, etc. By all means, invite children's participation in the cleanup and express your appreciation for their help. Remember, young children like to put things back into containers almost as much as they like to dump things out.

Be Prepared

Toddlers won't wait. As much as possible, have everything gathered and ready to go before gathering them for a special activity. Don't invite them to the snack table before the snack is there. Have all the art or cooking activity materials in the room and ready before beginning.

A Few Children at a Time

When you do an art or cooking activity, or anything that requires close supervision, it's best to do it with just two or three children at a time. It's much easier to put on smocks, wipe spills, and make the materials available, without causing a lot of waiting time for children. Cleaning up is immeasurably easier! Most important, you have a far greater opportunity to provide the "envelope of language" for the experience. You can talk about what each child is doing, and you have time to *listen* and allow him to talk.

What about the other children? If you have another adult working with you, he can play with and supervise the other children. Have other equally interesting things for them to do. Some teaching teams take half the children outside while one teacher remains inside doing a special project with the rest of the group. If you work alone with a smaller group of children make sure other safe and easy activity choices are available for non-participants, such as puzzles, play dough or fit-together toys. You, of course, have to keep one ear open and be able to jump up at a moment's notice.

Sometimes children crowd and push and are impatient to participate. This usually happens when this is a new procedure. Simply explaining, "You will have a turn as soon as

Billy is finished," is usually sufficient. You could also suggest, "You can stand over here and watch if you want to, or you can play over there and I will call you when it is your turn." Once children gain confidence that they will indeed have a turn, the problem usually lessens.

You might worry that some children might not get a chance to do the activity if only a few at a time participate. Surprisingly, this is rarely the case. Your preparation and cleanup time is so reduced that there is usually plenty of time for all children who want to do it. You can always repeat the activity the next day. Ask yourself, "Why am I doing this with children?" If there is any learning value in a project, it's worth doing with a small number of children at a time.

Allow Them to Watch

Often non-participants will want to stand to the side and watch the action. There is nothing wrong with this as long as they have other choices of activities as well. Children can learn a lot by watching others engaged in an activity. It gives them "mental rehearsal" before they do it themselves.

Invite "Repeats"

"Read it again!" is a common phrase of two-year-olds when they have heard a story they like. "Do it again!" is too. If at all possible, ask a child if they would like to do another painting, or hear the song again, or throw the ball again. Don't worry about boring the child. He will tell you when it is enough and he is ready for something new. Toddlers and twos are good at "self-imposed drill," practicing actions and new skills over and over again. Never hesitate to repeat favorite activities. It is part of their "mastery" behavior – a prime way they learn.

Make Magic Story Rugs

Collect small carpet samples (free from carpet stores). Place these in a circle on the floor (or in whatever arrangement you want children to be seated). Seat each child on one carpet sample. This seems to be amazingly helpful in keeping children seated. It defines their own space and there is less kicking and shoving. You can thus make sure each child is in a position where he can see.

Bring Things to Life

Toddlers are tickled when you give human-like characteristics to non-human things. This is why so many children's books feature talking animals. It is why puppets have such appeal. *Goodnight Moon,* the book where the child says goodnight to everything in the room, is a true reflection of reality. Young children often talk to chairs, toys, spoons, and the like.

You can take advantage of this phenomenon in your teaching by having inanimate objects talk to the group, telling their life story and social significance. Conjure up a strange voice and hold up a banana and launch into a monologue: "Hello boys and girls. I am a banana. My name is Benny. I have thick yellow skin that's fun to unwrap. See these little brown spots on my tummy – that means I'm ripe and good to eat, etc., etc., etc." (Of course, you might have trouble getting kids to eat Benny once they've made friends with him!)

Employ a Pet Puppet

How would you like an assistant who will captivate children at group time, cut your cleanup time in half, keep children calm and interested while you're waiting for lunch, help tuck children in at nap time, greet children in the morning, bring out the shy child, help children work out social conflicts and greatly reduce problems? Skillful use of a "pet puppet" can accomplish all of these things.

Although there are many puppets available to buy that would fill the bill, the very best pet puppets are homemade sock puppets. The mouth of a sock puppet opens and closes and its face changes expressions as you move your hand inside, lending extra realism. You can give your pet puppet a real personality with accessories such as hair and eyelashes, a special voice, and of course, a name. He could have a special "house" (a box or fancy bag) to nap in when not in use.

It is a little disturbing to the ego, but children will pay attention to a puppet much longer than to an adult. It can teach concepts: "Put the ball *under* the chair, *behind* the chair." "Find things in the pile that are *blue*." It can organize children at cleanup time, help them, and encourage them. You'll be amazed at how much eager cooperation children give your puppet! The promise of a special kiss from the puppet and a little one-to-one conversation will get children settled more quickly at nap time. A puppet sings great lullabies to individual children, too. You could have a number of puppets who are specialists. One could lead games, one recite poetry, one tell stories, one teach songs, and others entertain at lunch, direct cleanup time, etc.

Make Transitions Predictable and Fun

Moving toddlers from one place to another can be a job! There are some techniques that help. The most significant thing you can do is to keep your routine consistent from day to day. Young children have only a very vague sense of time, but they do have a sense of the *order* of events. If you always have a story time after snack time, children will automatically assemble in your story place. The order of the particular events doesn't matter as much – just the consistency from day to day. Toddlers are real conservatives. They don't like change.

It also helps to talk about what's going to happen next. "In a few minutes we will go inside and take off our coats. Then we will eat lunch."

Sing Songs for Routines

Music is good for signaling routines. One caregiver plays march music at cleanup time. It's fun to make up simple songs to signal various aspects of your routine such as snack time, cleanup time, putting on coats, going inside, lunch, nap, etc. These have the melody cue as well as the words to tell them what to do. For example (to the the tune of "London Bridge"):

Now it's time to have our snack,
Have our snack,
Have our snack,
Now it's time to have our snack,
Come sit down.

Make sure you use different melodies for each song of your routine.

Beat the Doldrums

Late in the day is often a time when children are cranky and hard to please. Double that if it has been impossible for them to go outside and run off steam because of bad weather. Create a "Beat the Doldrums Kit" for such times. Put special toys in it to bring out only at that time. These don't have to be expensive or elaborate...just different. Some possibilities: special dress up clothes such as fancy hats, a feather boa, pretty scarves; stickers, old greeting cards, colored tape; a collection of spray can tops and jar lids for building; a box of pipe cleaners to bend into shapes; perhaps a small flashlight. If you are a parent anticipating a trip with a toddler, this type of thing can be a life-saver.

Choose Your Timing

Like anyone else, toddlers will be less ready to sit and listen if they are groggy from sleep early in the morning, tired at the end of the day, hungry, or otherwise not feeling tip top. If they are insecure or upset, if they are new to your group, if strangers are in the room, if it was a frantic morning before arriving, if there are distractions such as other children doing something exciting, if there is loud music elsewhere, or a thunderstorm, etc., we cannot expect the concentration of toddlers.

Use Humor

Have you ever been in a gathering in which an adult told an "adult humor" joke and a toddler present joined in with the hearty laughter of everyone else? This points out the most basic use of humor in our species – social bonding. There is something about laughing together that pulls us close to each other. There is no greater friendship builder than humor. But what is funny to toddlers? Novelty, surprise, and incongruity.

- **Peek-a-boo.** The game of peek-a-boo with all its variations is an example of surprise, and is sure to elicit smiles and laughter.

- **Incongruity** combines novelty and surprises. For all of us, something askew, not quite right, can tickle the funny bone. Animals that talk and wear clothing in children's books appeal for this reason – it's different enough to keep the attention of children. That's why making a puppet, doll, or banana talk will bring interest and smiles from children. All of this implies that the child knows what the real thing should look or act like.

- **Mistakes.** Toddlers enjoy doing something "wrong" like putting their shoes on their hands or wearing a pot for a hat. You could make mistakes in familiar songs. Sing "Old MacDonald had a duck..." but this duck says, "moo!" You can be sure someone in the group will say, "No way!" setting the stage for humor and delight.

- **Silliness.** The word "silly" seems to be a favorite of two-year-olds. Maybe because they're just figuring out what's factual, ordinary, or "not-silly," they take delight in the unusual. A two-year-old boy often comes up to his caregiver and just says, "You're silly." (An invitation for social interaction if there ever was one!) Asking children to show you a silly face makes them laugh. And they love silly rhyming songs with nonsense words. Likewise, books with silly happenings or fun sounds to repeat have appeal. In the process children are learning to enjoy books and discover that you can find some laughs between the covers. They enjoy knowing that they are capable of recognizing the funny parts. Twos also enjoy chanting silly sounds that they pick up from each other.

Help Children with Separation

We are all aware of how frightening it can be for a toddler to be separated from his or her parents. Because they have so little abstract thinking, it is hard for them to imagine what the parent is doing while not in their presence. And they have no concept of time. Caregivers sometimes make the mistake of saying something like, "Mommy will be back soon." But several hours can seem like an eternity to the toddler. Finally, it is also an issue of power. The child may try every trick in his repertoire to keep his parent from leaving — sad eyes, hugging, crying, screaming — and it still doesn't work. The child can feel utterly helpless and defeated. Here are some things that can help.

- **Rehearsal and familiarity.** When a child is to be put into child care outside the home for the first time, it helps tremendously if the parent and the child can visit ahead of time to become familiar with the place and with the person who will care for him. It's ideal if the parent can visit as often as necessary for the child to absorb the idea that this is a safe and fun place to be. Then the parent can rehearse being away, first leaving for just a few minutes and coming back and gradually increasing the length of time.

- **Send home a picture book.** Create a picture book using photos of the children and staff in your group, the routines of your day, some of your great toys, and fun activities you do together. Encourage the parents to read this to the child before starting in your program and anticipate all the fun he'll have.

- **Give a joyful greeting.** Be genuinely glad to see the child and the parent. Call them by name. Get the other children to come over and greet them too. Make the child feel like a welcome celebrity.

- **Encourage a good-bye ritual.** Let the parent and the child develop a consistent set of things they do to say good-bye, such as read one book, say hi to the guinea pig, kiss, rub noses, and then wave good-bye through the window. This gives the child a sense of control.

- **Picture routines.** Create a picture chart of the routines of the day, using photographs. Explain this to the child. Then show the child the point at which his parent will return. "See, here we go outside after snack time in the afternoon. Your daddy will come and get you while we are out there." Encourage parents to be as consistent as possible in their pick-up times.

- **Have pictures from home.** Laminate a picture or two that parents supply of their family, pets, and people who love them. Put these on a large key ring and allow the child to carry it around with him, or keep it in his cubby.

- **Objects from home.** Some children are comforted by having something they think their parent values – like an extra set of car keys or an old wallet. They may think, "Surely Mom won't forget me now, because she'll need her keys."

- **Pretend to call.** The child can use a toy telephone to pretend to call Mom or Dad at work. You can role-play the voice of the parent. "Hi Mark. I'm at work now. What are you playing with? What did you have for snack? I miss you too. I'll be there to get you after your nap this afternoon. Bye."

Transitional Objects – A Little Comfort from Home

Little Marjorie clutches her special dolly close to her as she faces the new day in your program. You can almost see her draw strength and courage out of that piece of cotton and polyester stuffing. You get a frantic call from parents at 8 p.m. Jason left his blankie at the center and he can't possibly go to sleep without it. Theodore, who has been playing busily all morning, suddenly panics when he realizes he is out of arm's reach of his bear. Calm is restored as you tell him it is in his cubby and he can get it if he needs it.

Transitional objects seem to take hold at the end of the infant year when the child is starting to walk and has two hands free for hauling things while he explores. These objects take on all different forms. Often it is the classic blanket, sometimes worn to shreds. Or it might be a stuffed animal or doll, threadbare from so much loving. Usually the object carries with it a particular smell, comforting to the child, dubious to the rest of us, and he allows the objects to be washed only after much cajoling and reassuring. The interesting thing is

nobody *taught* the child to use this object in this way. It seems to echo some basic instinct. Other primate babies hang onto mother and ride around on her back for much of their childhood. A blanket or stuffed animal is a "piece of home" – a symbol of mother – for the child to carry with him as he faces the wider world.

There are some children who don't have one particular transitional object, but are satisfied to have anything from home with them. Some children are content simply to have the object in their cubby where they can get at it if they need it. Other children literally panic if they are more than an arm's reach away from their object. The child will not need this emotional crutch forever. As he starts to feel more secure and adventurous, the blanket will be laid aside briefly. You can help him put it in his cubby where it will often remain for most of the day, only to be brought out at nap time. This is almost immediate with some children, and may take a long time with others.

As we think about ways to bridge the gap from home to school, let's also think about ways to bridge the gap the other way. Allow the child to take a little piece of you or your program home with him. Some programs have developed toy lending libraries. You could send a photo of you and the other children home with the child.

You might work toward having the child leave a special object from home at the center, and not taking it home every night. And have him use it mainly at nap time when it seems to be most necessary. This gives parents one less thing to find and pack in the morning, and often does the trick to make the child feel comfortable.

Pacifiers can pose special problems, and yet, children should be allowed to have them. Work on limiting when the child uses one. One caregiver told the children they could not bring them to their circle or story time. It's hard to talk when you're sucking on something. Encourage the child to put his pacifier in his cubby for when he really needs it, but not go around with it all day, because it impedes his expressive language development. Pacifiers also pose a hygiene problem. Caregivers wash them off with soap and water periodically and let them air dry. Use a permanent marker to put the child's name on the handle of the pacifier, to make sure that it gets back to the right child.

Not all children have transitional objects. They may deal with their anxiety in different, self-comforting ways, such as thumb sucking, hair twirling, "acting out" aggressively, or just crying. The ones with the transitional objects might just be the lucky ones.

PART II

—

ACTIVITIES

CHAPTER 4

Chanting, Naming, Listening, Talking

Caregivers of toddlers are interpreters. A child who was just beginning to form sentences said indistinctly, "Come over here." The caregiver said, "Jamie, did you hear Robbie? He said he wants you to come over here." The caregiver sat on the floor with some photographs of the children. Two children joined her. "Who's this? Why is she wearing a bathing suit?" She also talked directly to one child, an older two-year-old. "What's the matter?" The child pointed. The caregiver said, "You need to tell Robbie. Say, 'That's mine. I'm playing with that now.'" The child repeated those words to the offender and, amazingly, the toy was given back. Another outcry was heard. The caregiver said, "Jamie, do you hear what Kimmie is saying? She said, 'Mine!' She has that chair now. Here's one for you." A child brought over a torn book and held it up to her. The caregiver said, "Oh, I see this page is torn. Do you want me to tape it together?" He nodded. "Okay, let's go and get the tape." At snack time she asked, "What kind of juice do you think this is?" Child: "Applepine." Caregiver: "Oh, pineapple — yes, I think you're right."

What this all boils down to is being "tuned in" to children and aware of their efforts at communication and how to expand on them.

The use of language for communication is said to be one of the things that distinguishes humans from other living things on the planet. Toddlers are becoming more "human" every day as they acquire language at a dizzying speed. The baby of one year uttering a few single words (like "mine!" and "no!") will turn three with hundreds, even thousands of words at her command, putting together short sentences, and will have mastered most grammatical patterns of her native language. With the acquisition of language comes a capacity for more abstract thought.

As you know, toddlers are great imitators. The first thing a young child does is imitate the rhythm and melody and individual sounds of a language without putting together actual words. (Just like you can probably "imitate" Italian, say, without using actual words or knowing the language.) This stage of language development is called the "jargon" stage. As a child plays you will hear her carry on a very intelligent-sounding dialog totally in nonsense syllables. When children put together a string of nonsense syllables in their typical babbling, it's not as useless as it might seem. They are giving practice to the muscles which produce the sounds of our language. They are also using the typical rhythm and intonation patterns of the language they hear spoken around them. Gradually, more and more words will creep into this jargon.

UNDERSTANDING COMES FIRST

It is important to know that children understand many words and phrases before they can actually say them. It is for this reason that adults should talk to babies from the very beginning, but especially as they approach toddlerhood. The big, interesting world is out there, ready for their exploration. When they discover that things and actions have sounds attached to them, they are that much more eager to explore. So, don't feel silly having a conversation with a toddler!

NON-VERBAL LANGUAGE

Realize that language involves much more than words. Language is about communicating – having the ideas in one head register in another head. Non-verbal communication – gestures, tone of voice, facial expressions and squawks with intonation – comes long before actual words. In fact, young toddlers can be very effective in communicating their wants and needs. When people respond appropriately, they are learning that this is one way to gain power, or that there is a *reason* to try to communicate. So, let a child know she has communicated. And use gestures and facial expressions to go along with what you are saying to her.

"Uh-oh!" Rather than being a word, this is more of an intonation. Many languages use this same intonation to notify that something is amiss. Because toddlers spill things and knock things over so much, they learn this expression very early. Since it usually generates some action or attention, many toddlers develop an uh-oh game. Sometimes they say "uh-oh" *before* they dump something. It's a warning...act fast!

LABELING

It seems to be with great satisfaction that toddlers will point to objects or pictures and name them...as if to say, "I know what that is!" One word utterances, "chair," "doggy" come before whole sentences. They also learn how to get the services of adults by pointing to things and saying, "Whassat?"

THE ENVELOPE OF LANGUAGE

- Surround everything children do with meaningful language. Describe their actions, what they are holding and playing with, the sounds you are hearing, how others are feeling. Attaching real words to what a child is experiencing helps her vocabulary grow.

- Expand on a child's language. If a child points to the juice pitcher and grunts, instead of just pouring the child some juice you can say, "Oh, I see you want more juice. I will pour you some in your glass." At this point you are translating grunts. Soon you can encourage the child to use words rather than grunts, and you can expand on single word utterances. Child: "Crayons!" Caregiver: "You want to color with crayons, Joey? Okay, I'll get you a piece of paper and you can sit next to Rachel."

BE A GOOD LANGUAGE MODEL

- Gear your language to be just one step above the child's ability. Many parents do this naturally and there is even a term for this type of language – "motherese," or "parentese."

- Toddlers need "straight talk" in a normal tone of voice and a fairly slow pace.

- Pronounce words correctly and use good grammar.

- Use full sentences whenever you can. When a child asks, "What's that?" rather than answering, "A garbage truck," respond, "That is a garbage truck."

- As much as possible use nouns instead of pronouns. Say, "Roll the *ball*," instead of "Roll *it*." "Put the *puzzles* on the *shelf*," rather than "Put *them* over *there*."

- Be as specific as possible about location words too. "The pegs are on the bottom shelf beside the puzzles." Contrast the language learning possibilities of the above sentence to a reply where you simply point in the general direction and say, "Over there."

- Naturally, children make numerous mistakes as they acquire standard speech patterns. Instead of correcting a child directly, simply reflect the phrase back to the child as a natural part of your own speech, in its correct form. For instance, if a child says, "Her done it," reply, "Yes, Jason, she did it."

It takes practice and a conscious effort to speak with such clarity. You'll find it does get easier.

CHILDREN LEARN BEST FROM REAL EXPERIENCES

Give children a broad base of experience. Seeing a real cow will have more meaning than looking at a picture and being taught to say, "cow." Taking short trips to interesting places and providing many things to handle and examine will be very valuable.

While children mainly learn language from real interactions that happen during their day, there are many simple games and activities to give toddlers experience with words and expand their receptive and productive vocabularies.

Chanting Back and Forth

Toddlers do a lot of "chanting" to themselves as they play – often a rhythmic repetition of several syllables. "Do-da-do-da-do-da..." If you hear this, try to pick up on it and mimic it along with the child in a playful sing-song way.

You can do this in reverse. Produce your own simple rhythmic chant while you're sitting on the floor playing with a child. Pause and look expectantly at the child and see if she mimics your chant. Vary your intonation to a question mode and back to a statement mode. You are teaching the child to play with sounds which will eventually lead to more flexibility and capability with real words.

Hollering

Cut the large end off a bleach bottle and wash it out thoroughly. You have a megaphone. (Children will also enjoy looking through both ends, or it may become a hat.)

Where Is It?

Name things in the room and see if the child can point to them or go over to them. Use real objects. You could have a puppet do the asking. Toddlers love to perform for a puppet. "Where is the rocking chair?"

As you're going for a walk outside, say, "I see a tricycle. Do you see a tricycle?" If the child points to it, go on to another item. If not, point to it yourself or go over to it. She will catch on.

Match Pictures to Objects

Mount drawings or magazine pictures of real objects in the room on large cardboard cards. Cover them with clear self-adhesive paper. Hand a card to the child and say, "This is a picture of an orange. Can you find the real orange in the room?" Have the child take the picture over to the real object.

Find It in the Picture

Let the child find objects in pictures on a magazine page or picture book page. At first concentrate on nouns..."things." As the child gains skill you can ask her to find examples of descriptive adjectives or action words. "Find something *soft*." "Find something that is *flying*."

Body Parts

Have a child point to and later name body parts on herself, a doll, an image in a mirror, in pictures, or on you. With older toddlers talk about the function of the body part. "Point to what the doggie eats with," "hears with," etc.

What's That?

You point to an object or a picture of an object, ask "What's that?" and see if the child can name the object. The child must produce the word, not you. Toddlers seem to find great enjoyment in this activity. Once they get the idea that certain combinations of sounds represent particular objects they seem to be on an endless quest to learn more words and proudly pronounce them. They have entered the "productive" stage of language development.

Nursery Rhymes

Traditional "Mother Goose" rhymes as well as some more contemporary poetry delight toddlers. These rhymes play with sounds, just the way toddlers do. Don't worry if children don't understand all of the words. "Deedle, deedle, dumpling, my son John..." "Hickory dickory dock..." Phrases like these are fun to say and are musical and rhythmical in effect.

- Chant these rhymes as you push children on the swing, wait for lunch, change diapers, clap your hands with a small group of children and at other odd moments of the day.

- Try leaving off the last words of lines of familiar rhymes and see if children will say them.

- Clap while you say the rhymes, to emphasize their rhythm.

- Sing the melodies for the rhymes, also emphasizing their timing and rhyming sounds.

- Have drawings of characters from the rhymes for your flannel board. See if children can identify what rhyme the drawing represents.

- Find dress-up clothes that represent characters in the rhymes.

Fingerplays

Two-year-olds enjoy simple fingerplays (poems accompanied

by simple hand movements) such as "Eensie Weensie Spider" or "Twinkle, Twinkle Little Star." Some will only kind of "half do it" but they enjoy involving their hands and body with making sounds. You can make it very simple by having only one cue for them to listen for – such as crouching down and waiting for the word, "Pop!" to jump up in "Pop Goes the Weasel." There are many fingerplay books on the market and in libraries.

Flannel Board Progression

The flannel board is a good tool to use with toddlers because it holds their attention. They are fascinated by the magic that makes things stick to it. And you have endless variety. Just cut pictures out of magazines, put clear self-adhesive paper on the front and felt on the back.

Step 1 – Introducing.
> You have four or five pictures. Name each one as you put it on the flannel board. "This is a cat." "This is a duck."

Step 2 – Comprehension.
> Have a child point to the object you name. "Which one is the cow?" She could either pick the cow from pictures on the floor and put it on the board for you, or take it off the board and put it in the box for you.

Step 3 – Production of speech.
> You ask, "What's this?" If the child correctly names the object you point to she can put it on the board or take it off.

Puppet Packs a Bag

Your pet puppet announces that she's going on a trip to spend the weekend at her grandmother's house (or wherever). She brings out a little suitcase, which will in itself be fascinating to the toddler. Then she solicits the toddler's help in finding the items to put in her suitcase. "Bring me the yellow ball." "Now I need a cup." "I have to have a book." "Bring me something soft."

Matching Cards

With this game you are working on the concept of "same and different" as well as building vocabulary. Buy two of the same issue of a magazine. Cut out the same pictures from each magazine. Make pairs of cards from these by gluing them onto cardboard and covering them with clear self-adhesive paper. Then mix up a bunch of these and spread them out on the table top or floor in front of the child. Hold one up and ask, "Can you find one the **same** as this?" Or, "Look, I found a cat. Can you find a picture of a cat just like this?" Later the child will be able to play this independently. You could also have children match pairs of identical small objects, fabric swatches, or paint samples.

Simple Picture Lotto

The only difference between a lotto game and matching cards

is that lottos have several pictures on one larger board and individual pictures to match to the ones on the board. Make them the same way. Three or four pictures on the larger board will be enough for toddlers. You could take advantage of the game design and have a different "category" on each board. For instance, have three pictures of dogs on one, three cats on another, and three pictures of babies on a third board.

Picture File

Develop an ever-growing picture file – a collection of interesting pictures cut out of magazines, glued to a piece of construction paper, and covered with clear self-adhesive paper. You can use the pictures in various ways as children get older, stimulating new levels of language and thought development.

Show a child one picture at a time and let her tell you about it. You can ask some open-ended questions like, "What's going on here?" "Why do you think he looks sad?"

You can expand the child's understanding of categories by finding many variations of things – many different kinds of birds, for instance. (Of course, children learn best by seeing the real thing, but pictures will reinforce their understandings.)

Children of about two can do simple sorting. Have a collection of two kinds of things – for instance, cars and dogs. Say, "I got these all mixed up. Would you put the pictures of cars over here and the pictures of dogs over there?"

Greeting Cards

Ask parents and friends to give you their old greeting cards. Toddlers love them any time of year. They can be a good transition tool. Hand them out to children if they have to wait for some reason. You can add good pictures to your picture file, or put backing on them for your flannel board.

OTHER ACTIVITIES INVOLVING HEARING

"Wow! What a loud truck!" "Listen, do you hear the birds?" "Who is that laughing? It sounds like Susan, doesn't it?" Your "envelope of language" will help develop a child's awareness of sounds and auditory discrimination, which is ultimately important for language development and later learning to read.

Go on a Sound Walk

Give children a small stick like an unsharpened pencil. Let them tap all kinds of things in the room and/or outside to see what kind of sound it makes.

Tape Recorder Fun

Record familiar sounds and see if children can identify them. Possibilities: a car starting, dog barking, vacuum cleaner, dish washer, horn honking, toilet flushing, doorbell, someone knocking on the door, telephone ringing, the Sesame Street theme song, and voices of familiar people.

FREQUENTLY ASKED QUESTIONS

Will it hurt a child's language development if the caregiver speaks with an accent or uses bad grammar?

Generally, no. The caregiver will not be the child's only language model. Naturally, those who work with very young children should try their best to use good grammar, and make efforts to improve if there is a problem. Try to pair up the caregiver with an accent with one who has standard pronunciation.

What about learning a second language, or hearing two languages in infancy?

Young children have an amazing capacity to learn a second language. It does not hurt them in any way; in fact, it can be a wonderful advantage, giving the child's brain that much more flexibility. Even if a child forgets a language learned in infancy, it will be easier to learn later on. However, the language should be learned by exposure to a real person speaking that language and playing and interacting with the child. Listening to recordings of people speaking in a different language has little value.

How can I tell if a child has a hearing problem?

You can't, for sure. Certainly, all toddlers have pronunciation inaccuracies. Because of the frequency with which children under three get head colds and ear infections, young children are at high risk for suffering temporary or permanent hearing losses. If you suspect that the child is not hearing properly, recommend that she be tested by her pediatrician or a hearing specialist. Many county health departments conduct free hearing screenings for young children. A hearing loss can have severe detrimental effects on the child's ability to learn, so don't ignore these signs that there may be a problem:

- The child has little productive language compared to others her age.

- The child's pronunciation is way off.

- The child's tone of voice is very loud, nasal, or monotonal.

CHAPTER 5

Reading Picture Books — Purchased and Homemade

*S*ixteen-month-old Terisa selects a book from her extensive *library and brings it over to her waiting grandfather's lap. Together, they "play" with the book. She opens it to a page with a dog. "Gog!" she says, and he repeats, "Dog!" She turns the page and says, "Bye, bye, gog." Then she flips the page back again and says, "Hi, gog!" They go on to do this with other pages in the book, greeting and saying bye-bye to the pictures.*

Most toddlers love books. A major part of the appeal is the *peek-a-boo* effect children get with books. Each page offers a new surprise. Toddlers like to play with anything resembling a hinge, and a book is really a hinge system. You'll often see a child flip a page back and forth to make the pictures appear and disappear.

Having many quality children's picture books in your environment and reading them to the child or children in your care often has the added advantages of increasing vocabulary, and actually helping to shape the child's brain to be receptive to language. So it's important to read to children from early infancy on. It's critical that a child in our society becomes literate, so we should think about how to create in children a disposition to love books.

BENEFITS OF READING TO TODDLERS AND TWOS

- **Emotional.** When a child can snuggle up with a parent or favorite caregiver and enjoy a book together, he is learning that books = pleasure. Learning happens in the context of emotion.

- **Social conditioning.** Toddlers are imitators. When the child sees adults enjoying books and attractive books are a familiar and regular part of the environment, the child will absorb the idea that this is what people do. They read.

- **Pro-social.** It is hard for young children to share. But a book is one thing they can share successfully. The adult can use the word "share" consciously. "I have a book here that I really like, and I'm going to share it with you now."

- **Paying attention.** Learning to focus attention on one thing and screen the rest of the room out is an important skill. More and more children are easily distracted in our over-stimulating world. Early experiences with books could possibly provide early success experiences to build on.

- **Using symbols.** Children gain experience using picture symbols – seeing that the image on the paper represents something real. Later the child will be able to use more abstract symbols – words made of letters.

- **Sequencing.** Initially, toddlers dive into a book in the middle and look at it backwards and upside down. But eventually they learn that a book and the story within have a beginning, middle and end.

- **Exposure to aesthetics.** Picture books are an art form in themselves. Much fine art is available in beautiful illustrations and photography. You can expose children to many different styles.

- **Imagination.** The root word of imagination is *image*. When you expose children to rich language and beautiful images, you are giving them imagination fodder.

TECHNIQUES FOR READING TO THIS AGE GROUP

It can be hard to keep the attention of a busy toddler. Young toddlers will try to grab the book from you and turn the pages faster than the story goes. Often people get into the most trouble reading to toddlers when they try to emulate a "circle time" of a preschool classroom. While children will often sit still in a group and enjoy a good book, don't necessarily expect this all the time. They need active involvement.

- **Start with an object.** You might find an object that relates to the topic of the book. This is sure to attract the attention of object loving toddlers. Talk about it for a minute or two and then say, "I just happen to have a book about (the object)."

- **Establish a reading routine.** Read at certain times each day. Don't limit reading to bedtime or naptime. Establish several times in your daily routine when children can expect a book, such as right after snack time, or as soon as you come in from outside. It's a good way to calm down at the end of the day as well.

- **Flop and Do.** From time to time, simply flop down on the floor with a book and see who shows up. "I love this book…want to look at it with me?"

- **One-on-one snuggle.** When you get a chance, cozy up with just one child to read a book. It will make him feel special and he will absorb the emotional benefit of really enjoying a book at his own pace.

- **Follow the interest of the child.** The child will often have some comment about what he sees on the page. Follow the child's lead. While you want to move the story along, let him be actively involved. That's probably even more important. Remember your goal is to promote a love of books, so create as few negatives as possible. This is easiest, of course, when reading to a child one-on-one.

- **Spontaneous reading.** If a child brings you a book, and you can, drop what you're doing and read.

- **Adjust and simplify.** Use "parentese" when you read a book to a child, simplifying the language, slowing down, responding, and expanding on the words as needed.

- **Repetition.** Read books again and again. Often when you finish a book children will request, "Read it again!" Comply if you can. And keep familiar favorite books around. They like the predictability of that, like greeting old friends.

- **Show your own interest and enthusiasm in books.** Say things like "This is one of my favorite books." "I love the pictures in this book." "I found a book I thought you would love."

- **Have a library area in the room.** You're setting aside books as something special. You are also teaching children to take good care of books by placing them carefully on a shelf.

- **Encourage children to share books from home.** If you are in a child care or play group setting, make this the exception to your "no toys from home" rule. And share with parents what you know about quality books and give them book lists. (Parents are very receptive to this.)

- **Give them a rest.** Put some of your books away for several weeks. When you bring them out again, children will greet them like old friends and have renewed interest.

CHOOSING GOOD BOOKS FOR TODDLERS AND TWOS

There are more and more excellent books available for very young children. Unfortunately, there are a lot of mediocre ones as well. Use what you know about the children and what they are interested in to help you select good ones.

- **Sturdy construction.** Board books are best for young toddlers. The pages don't tear so easily and are easier for the children to turn. But make sure that the content is right for toddlers, and is not simply a board book conversion of a book designed for older children. Board books are better than cloth books. The pages are easier to turn and the quality of the illustrations is far superior.

- **Simplicity in images.** Picture books with one object or idea on a page are very good first books to start children naming objects. You should look for simplicity and clarity of illustrations and photographs, as well as their general attractiveness.

- **Rich language.** Look for books with beautiful words as well as beautiful pictures, words with rich sounds, rhythms and rhyme.

- **Familiar subjects.** Find books that reflect the child's world

– things he is likely to recognize and things he is interested in. Babies, animals, families, vehicles and household objects are possibilities.

• **Respectful representations.** Find books that represent a wide variety of people, but represent them respectfully.

• **Interesting pictures.** Children around 2-1/2 years old with slightly longer attention skills and an expanding vocabulary like "busy" pictures with many different things on a page. It's fun to play the "Where Is It?" game with such books.

• **Humor.** Children like funny noises, surprises, funny images that invite sound effects.

• **Interesting characters and situations.** Young children seem to like animal characters. Perhaps the child can identify with the animal stories easier than with people characters who are obviously not themselves. Look for stories and characters that capture their interest.

• **Repetition and predictability.** Look for books with repeated phrases that children can chime in on and a pattern of action that makes the story somewhat predictable. This gives children a feeling of capability. They know what's going to happen.

• **Simple stories.** As children approach three years old they will be able to listen to simple stories.

• *You* **love it.** Collect books you personally love to read to children and you'll find yourself doing it more often.

CURRICULUM EXTENSIONS

You can extend the child's interest in a book and what he learns from it by designing activities that relate to the book.

Possibilities:

- **Objects.** Find objects represented in the book for children to play with.

- **Dramatic play.** Find props and dress-up clothes that relate to the book for children to use, such as different sizes of bowls and chairs for "The Three Bears." You could also help the children act out parts of the story, such as the Billy Goats Gruff going over a bridge.

- **Miniature play.** A child could use small people and vehicles to represent what happened in a story.

- **Puppets.** Your puppet could ask the children about the book. Or you might find, or dress up, a puppet to represent one or more of the characters, such as in the "Red Riding Hood" story. The puppet could then pause and tell the children how she was feeling when certain things happened.

- **Sing.** Make up a song about the book, or sing melodies relating to rhymes in familiar nursery rhyme books.

- **Cook.** Some books, such as "The Little Red Hen," lend themselves easily to fun cooking projects.

- **Recite.** When a book is *very* familiar to you and the children, recite the words while doing other things, such as swinging on the swing or riding in the car.

HOMEMADE BOOKS

Even with the wealth of beautiful children's picture books available, it's a good idea to have homemade books available as well. You can tailor the subjects to things you know a particular child is interested in. If a child sees you making books and has a part in it, he will feel all the more capable around books.

Homemade books for toddlers need to be sturdy and able to withstand wear and tear. It is important to teach children a respect for books from the very beginning and not allow them to tear pages. But toddlers' hand motions are not always going to be gentle so it's best to make pages that will not easily be destroyed. Stiff pages are easier for toddlers to turn and the hinge action of the pages fascinates them.

Homemade books are such fun to make and provide such enjoyment you'll probably end up with quite a collection before long.

Zip Lock Bag Books

These are fun to make, and very versatile. Simply take several small zip lock bags and sew them together along the bottom edge opposite the zip lock closing to make "pages" for your book. A regular overcast stitch works fine, or you can sew them together using a zig zag stitch on a sewing machine. Now cut some cardboard to just fit inside the bags. (This makes the pages stiff and easier to turn.) Then find magazine pictures or photos to slip on either side of the cardboard. You can change these pictures as often as you like, giving the child frequent variety.

Looseleaf Notebook Picture Book

Purchase a small (5" x 8") ring binder. Glue magazine pictures on both sides of a piece of construction paper or thin posterboard. Punch holes with a hole puncher and reinforce the holes with reinforcement rings. Then cover both sides of the pages with clear self-adhesive paper. Repunch the holes. Put several pages like this in the binder. You can change the pages as often as you like to keep interest high and emphasize certain concepts. It gives toddlers a very sturdy book which they can carry around and handle freely.

Photo Album Book

Put photos and magazine pictures under the magnetic plastic pages of a photo album. Again, these are stiff pages and it is easy to change the pictures. You might make a collection of pictures all of one type of thing, such as dogs or cars. A book with many pictures of babies is very popular with two-year-olds who are proud that they are no longer babies.

Sewn Paper Book

Assemble pages of pictures glued to construction paper and covered with clear self-adhesive paper. You will want two pictures, side by side on each side of each page. Vinyl wallpaper samples would make good covers. Put the wallpaper (cut to the same size as the paper) on the bottom. Sew right up the middle with a large stitch on a sewing machine.

Magazines As Picture Books

Magazines make good picture books for toddlers. They are full of pictures of things familiar to young children: kitchens, food, pets, children, and mommies. They will greatly enjoy sitting down and paging through a magazine with you.

Scrapbook

Develop a scrapbook of photographs and pictures of people and objects familiar to the child. This is a "real life" word book pertinent to that child. It will become a favorite book.

FREQUENTLY ASKED QUESTIONS

Children are destructive with books – how can we have them out without having them destroyed?

It's true that young toddlers have a heavy hand and can be rough with books. For this reason, the books you leave out for them to handle should be sturdy and made to hold up. However, it is possible to teach children to be careful with books. Show them how to turn the pages carefully by picking up the side of the page with thumb and forefinger rather than scraping with their whole hand. Praise the child when he does it right. Show him how to place the book on the shelf rather than leaving it on the floor and praise when he does this. If a book becomes torn, express concern and let the children watch as you carefully tape it back together. And, finally, it's okay to keep certain books "special" and bring them out only when you are there to supervise and help children handle them correctly.

When I try to read to him, he just grabs the book out of my hand and turns the pages.

This child is still exploring books as interesting objects. Allow him to do that, but name things on the pages he opens. He'll get used to the idea that books have lots of fun things inside and will eventually learn to settle down and hear the story.

My children have a wide range of language ability. How do I select a book to read that will be interesting to all of them?

You might let different children choose the book when you read to them. Adjust the language according to who is with you. And use the "flop and do" technique. Read to just one or two at a time for best results. A good book will appeal to children on several different levels so they can enjoy it over a long period of time.

CHAPTER 6

Singing, Dancing, Noise Making

*T*he children are playing randomly at numerous different play areas in the the room, but there have been a few "skirmishes" and"squawks" as they begin to push at each other and test limits. The caregiver, Nancy, grabs her guitar and flops down on the floor, playing a lively tune. All random action in the room stops and the children come over to her and jump up and down with big smiles on their faces.

"Move as the spirit moves you!" Toddlers certainly seem to know how to do this when they hear music. In fact, it is almost impossible for them not to move when a lively tune comes their way. Likewise, they love chiming in with their voices. Truly, music is a natural activity for this age. It's actually an extension of communication. Just as children babble and speak "jargon" with intonation patterns before they say actual words, children can sing before they can talk. Music is a social experience.

Since music communicates feelings even more directly than words, it's a good way to soothe a troubled child. It's rare in our society to be personally sung to. You can give children this gift. It can be a great way to express emotions.

Plan music as an activity with children, rather than just having it on as background music all day. That desensitizes children to music. But when you tell them, "I have some lovely music to play for you today...I think you will like to dance to it," you are focusing their attention and developing an appreciation and ability to enjoy music. Play and/or sing "live" music with children as well as play recorded music. Chant, sing, dance and clap with them. A musical environment helps generate musical children.

SINGING

Few toddlers can carry a tune, but they enjoy singing and you will notice that their voices go up and down in the right places when they are familiar with the song. "Ring Around the Rosie" and "Twinkle, Twinkle Little Star" are universal children's melodies in many different cultures, and they seem to be the easiest melodies for children to learn. Try chanting the "Ring Around the Rosie" melody singing, "na, na, na," instead of words. Do they match your tone? Sometimes the toddler will join in with a fairly accurate imitation. If you sing a lot, your toddlers will sing a lot.

There are many song books and recordings to choose from. Good songs for this age are simple, with easy rhythms and not requiring a wide vocal range. Traditional nursery rhyme melodies are a good place to start. Also make up your own songs about the routines of your day, your pets, what a child likes to do, etc.

To teach a song:

- Use a puppet or some interesting object related to the song to get their attention. (Puppets are great at teaching songs.)
- Sing the whole song so they can hear it all the way through.

- Say the words one line at a time and have them repeat it. (They are good mimickers so they can usually do this.)
- Then leave out a word. "Twinkle, twinkle, little …" and have them put in the word.
- Do the same thing singing the lines, one at a time.
- Then, combine – singing pairs of lines, and then the whole song.
- Remember, children don't learn a song from singing it once. They have to hear it many times.
- Keep it simple.
- Expect their attention for only seven or eight minutes.

Repeat this process, and sing the song as you go along numerous times during the day.

Different Tones of Voice

Once children are very familiar with a song, suggest singing it in different ways. Sing it in high, little voices, sing it whispering, sing it in loud, angry voices, like they are monsters, etc.

Add a Prop

Make a simple prop to go along with favorite songs such as green frog puppets to go along with "The Little Green Frog" song. A paper headband with a teddy bear could go along with teddy bear songs.

Cardboard Tube "Kazoo"

Cut a circle of wax paper about 5" in diameter. Attach this to
the end of a cardboard toilet paper tube with a rubber band.
Punch a small hole half way up the tube. Show children how
to sing into the end of this to make a tickly buzzing sound.
Can they sing the "Ring Around the Rosie" melody into it?

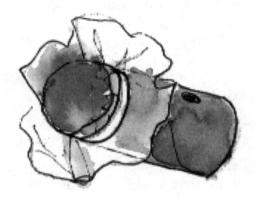

Personal Lullabies

As you tuck each child in at naptime, or bedtime at home,
sing a special lullaby using the child's name in it. You might
have several different lullabies for her to choose from. This
very personal gift will make the child feel special and cared
for. It doesn't have to be a traditional lullaby. "Rudolf the Red
Nosed Reindeer," with the child's name substituted for
"Rudolf," is a favorite.

A Few More Hints:

- If you have a very active group, try having children stand
  up while you sing together.
- Make motions with your body. Sway and turn.
- Sing a lullaby at the end of the music time to calm children
  down.
- If you do music before nap time, keep the songs calm.

DANCING

Put some music on and it's hard to *keep* toddlers from dancing! If you dance too, and move in different ways, your toddlers will dance even more. In the process they practice balance, coordination, and rhythm, and experience the pure pleasure of moving to music.

Hip Dancing

What toddlers love most of all is for adults to pick them up, sit them on their hips and dance to music.

"The Toddler Stomp"

The typical toddler "dance" is to rock side to side in a wide stance. Children often start doing this spontaneously when they hear some lively music. They also enjoy doing the "toddler stomp" holding hands with a partner. Good social interaction.

Shadow Dancing

Pull the curtains closed, take the shade off of a small lamp or use a slide projector, and place it on the floor at the side of the room so that it will cast shadows on the wall if children stand in front of it. Now put on some music and invite children to dance with their shadows. Great idea for a rainy day!

Things to Shake and Wave

Remember, toddlers love objects. Create things for them to shake or wave while they dance, such as paper pom poms, scarves or crepe paper streamers.

Stop the Music

Have the children dance while the music plays, fall down when it stops.

NOISE MAKING

Hand a toddler any new object and she will go through a series of test procedures. First it will go to the mouth to see how it tastes. Then she will probably turn it all around to examine all sides. Then, almost for sure, she will shake it up and down and bang it against a surface to see what kind of noise it makes. Since toddlers love to make things produce noises, it's a good idea to have a variety of noise makers and to make them available at a time when noise is acceptable.

You can, of course, buy rhythm instruments from equipment suppliers, but there are plenty of instruments that are easy and inexpensive to make, and are a big hit with toddlers. Here are a few samples.

Shakers

Toddlers will enjoy a wide variety of shakers. The primary pleasure in shakers is cause and effect. "I move my hand in this way and it makes a neat noise." Make a collection of all different types of cans with plastic lids: film canisters, potato chip cans, popcorn and nut cans, juice cans and coffee cans. Partially fill the cans with such things as salt, marbles, rice, beans, nuts and bolts, styrofoam squiggles. Glue the lids on well and decorate if you wish. Tape the edges, and keep in good repair.

A Shaker Collection

Even more fun than one shaker is lots and lots of shakers. Make a collection and keep it in a special box. "Look, I have all kinds of things in this box that make a noise when you shake them! Which one would you like to try first?" "Shake, shake, shake." "Oh, that makes a loud noise."

Matching Pairs

If you make pairs of shakers filled with the same thing, older toddlers will enjoy finding the matching can. Another variation is to use the small plastic Easter eggs. Fill their bottom halves with various substances to shake and glue them shut. These can be stored in an egg carton. Perhaps you can find two eggs each of six different colors and make those match sounds. Then the child will have the color clue as well as the sound clue to find matching pairs. This will also appeal to toddlers' compulsion to fit objects into spaces when they replace the eggs into the egg carton.

Washboard

A metal washboard (you can still get them in hardware stores) is fun to scrape with a wooden rod.

Twanger

An old fashioned door stop with a spring that sticks out of the wall makes a wonderful twanging noise when a child snaps it. You could attach one (or several) to a board, small wooden box, or the back of a shelf or room divider. Can the children imitate the noise it makes? Glue the rubber tips on securely.

Sandpaper Blocks

Glue sandpaper to one side of a small piece of wood or heavy cardboard measuring about 3" by 3". Attach a knob on the back for a handle or staple a strap or piece of elastic to form a loop on the back. Show the toddler how to slide these back and forth against each other to make a "brushing" sound.

Pots and Pans

Don't forget the all-time favorite kitchen pots and pans band. This can be the most fun of all. Join in and play with the cookie sheet gongs, wooden spoon rhythm sticks or drumsticks, pot drums, pot lid cymbals, and a metal spoon "ding-a-linging" inside a metal can.

Rock Band

Give each child two rocks. Let them bang them together to see what sound they make. When the whole group does this you are creating "music" of a unique sort.

Rhythm Sticks

Hardware stores and lumber yards sell different thicknesses of wooden dowels. They will probably cut them into shorter lengths for you. Different thicknesses and lengths produce different sounds. Have a variety, in pairs.

Wood Blocks

As for sandpaper blocks described above, cut two small pieces of wood about 3" by 4" and attach a small knob on the back of each. Sand the wood smooth to make sure there are no splinters. Let children clap them together.

Drums

Children will have a fine time banging on a coffee can or other large can which costs nothing. (Cover the rough edges on the open end with heavy tape or contact paper.) At least one good drum is a very nice thing to have because of the quality of the sound. Tambourines are also loved by toddlers.

Multi-Cans Drum

Tape together a number of empty cans of various sizes so they form a circle. Duct tape works well. Use the kind of can opener that does not leave sharp edges. Let the child bang on the various cans with a short stick and see what different sounds they make. An unsharpened pencil with a large rubber eraser glued on makes a good drum stick.

Bells

It would be fun to develop a collection of bells for toddlers to try. Counter bells – the kind you bang on in stores to get the attention of the clerk – are loved by toddlers. There are various jingle bell instruments available commercially. You could also securely sew jingle bells onto loops of elastic that can be slipped over the child's wrist. Small, unbreakable dinner bells, bicycle bells, and cow bells are other possibilities. Different hand actions are required to produce these fun sounds. Collect other kinds of non-breakable bells for children to play with. Each will produce its own unique sound. Keep this collection in a special box and bring it out when you can supervise.

Instruments *NOT* Recommended for Toddlers

Triangles, Cymbals, Hanging "Gongs"

Triangles and hanging gongs are too difficult for toddlers because you have to let the instrument hang freely with one hand, holding only the string hanger, and tap it lightly with the stick with the other hand. Toddlers find it difficult to coordinate two different hand actions and they generally want to grasp the metal part of the triangle and strike with that as well as the stick.

In order for cymbals to sound right you have to strike them lightly together and bring them apart immediately to let them vibrate. This is too complex for most toddlers. A couple of pot lids will be just as satisfying.

Some Things to Do with Instruments

With young toddlers you'll have to allow a great deal of time just to "free play" with the instruments. Don't have high expectations for structured performing.

Start with the Body as the First Rhythm Instrument

"Let's see what sounds we can make just using our bodies." Lead the group in all the variations of clapping you can think of. Clap with flat hands, cupped hands, just fingertips, the back of your hands, etc. Then try patting cheeks. What happens when you open your mouth and pat your cheeks? Pat the top of your head, your knees, the floor. Clap your knees. Rub flat hands together. What else can you think of? "Does it make a noise when we blink our eyes?" "How softly can you clap?" "How loudly can you clap?" "Can you clap slowly, like this?" "Can you clap real fast?" (Later try all of this with instruments.)

What Made That Sound?

Gather three or four different rhythm instruments or noise makers. Get a barrier of some sort to block children's view, such as a large box, piece of cardboard or your flannel board. Show children the instruments. Make a noise with each instrument and tell the children what the instrument is called. Hide the instruments behind the barrier. Play one of them. Let the children guess which instrument was played. Let them test their guess by playing the instrument they chose.

Don't expect toddlers or twos to march to music and play instruments at the same time. It's too difficult to do several things at once. In fact, keeping time to music with instruments or body movements is generally too difficult.

Multicultural Music

All cultures have music. It is a great way to add a multicultural component to your curriculum.

- Ask parents to share recorded music from their cultures.

- Invite a parent or friend from a different culture to visit and sing or play music from his or her culture to the children.

- Collect rhythm instruments from different cultures for children to use.

- Play recorded music from different cultures and invite children to dance to it.

FREQUENTLY ASKED QUESTIONS

I can't carry a tune, and I'm embarrassed when other adults hear me. Won't I be a bad example for children?

Don't worry! Children don't care! What you're getting across is the joy of music. What other adults will hear (with a smile perhaps) is someone who can communicate the pleasures that music offers. Also, there's lots you can do with music besides singing, such as dancing, using noise makers, etc.

Whenever I bring out rhythm instruments for children to play, no matter what instrument they have, they seem to want what the child next to them has.

It's much easier if you can give all the children the same instrument – another advantage of making your own inexpensive, homemade instruments. In addition to eliminating the fighting, it intensifies the sound and the children become more aware of the noises each type of instrument makes.

CHAPTER 7

Making Things Happen — Playing with Cause and Effect

*T*wo-year-old Nicole expresses outrage after stepping into a hotel elevator when some unthinking adult pushes the button to make it move. To make her feel better, her mother, not in a terrible hurry for once, lets her ride up and down several times, doing all the button pushing, before continuing with their errands.

Toddlers are fascinated by getting dramatic results from simple hand actions. "I wonder what would happen if..." seems to be the constant, unspoken question in their minds. They have discovered that they can make things happen. Power! We see this in their fascination with switching lights on and off, unrolling toilet paper, flushing toilets, ringing doorbells and knocking things over. Actually this process is the beginning of logical thought: action A causes response B. Our little scientists will test actions over and over to see if they produce the same results. You and I would probably do the same thing if we were suddenly placed on a new

planet. In order to act as independent beings we have to figure out how the world works so we can rely on ourselves and
not forever be dependent on others. Besides, making things
happen is fun! So, collect all kinds of things and activities that
cause interesting things to happen.

ACTIVITIES

Play Ball!

Toddlers are fascinated by all kinds of balls. Any kind of ball
play is a good "cause and effect" activity because an action
produces an immediate response. Vary the action, the
response varies.

Ideas:

- Show a small group of children or an individual child how
  to roll the ball back and forth with you. They will enjoy the
  social give and take as well as the action of the ball.

- Kicking a ball is a real challenge for toddlers because they
  have to balance on one foot to kick with the other foot.
  What pride when they can finally do it!

- Ask: "What else can you use to make the ball move? Can
  you bump the ball with your elbow? Try your knee."

- Develop a ball collection. A good collection of different
  sizes of balls is fairly inexpensive and will be much
  enjoyed by your toddlers. The popular foam rubber balls
  are great for indoor play but toddlers like to bite chunks
  out of them, so keep a watchful eye. Tennis balls, beach
  balls, footballs, and large rubber balls could be added.
  Keep them in a large laundry basket or a decorated cardboard box to facilitate cleanup.

- A very large rubber ball – one about 3 feet in diameter – is a great addition to your outside environment. Children love chasing it, rolling it and "spanking" it to make a great noise.

Marbles in a Tube

Get some flexible transparent tubing about one inch in diameter and about three feet long at the plumbing supplies department of your hardware store. Put several marbles inside the tube (the tube should be large enough so that they can roll freely) and glue corks securely in both ends of the tube. Cut the corks off even with the ends of the tube so a child 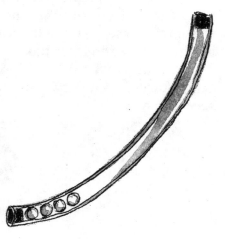 could not bite them off. Children see what happens to the marbles when they lift one end or the other or the middle.

Bubble in a Tube

Using about three feet of flexible transparent plastic tubing (see above), securely glue a cork into one end. Fill the tube with water you have colored with food coloring, leaving about one inch of air for a bubble. Glue a second cork into the other end. Cut the ends of the cork off to be even with the ends of the tube so a child could not bite them off. The child will enjoy watching the bubble travel up and down the tube when the ends are lifted.

Oil and Water Bottle

Find a sturdy transparent bottle such as a baby shampoo bottle and soak off the labels. Fill it about 1/3 full with water to which you have added some food coloring. Then fill the rest of the bottle almost to the top with mineral oil or baby oil. (Any kind of oil works – these are suggested only because they are colorless.) Glue the top on securely with quick bonding glue. Wiggling or shaking this bottle produces beautiful waves and slowly floating colored bubbles. A simple hand action produces a very pretty effect. This activity tends to be soothing as well.

More Bottle Shakers

Small plastic soft drink bottles make great "shake-shake" toys because children can see what is making the noise inside. Soak off the labels. Use all different kinds of materials inside such as popcorn kernels, buttons, jingle bells, and paper confetti. Glue the tops on securely. In some of them put things that don't make any noise when they are shaken, such as yarn pieces or little pom pom trims. You could also put colored water with dish detergent added so children can produce bubbles when it is shaken.

Roly-Poly Toys

Fill a plastic egg bottom with plaster of Paris. (These hollow colored eggs are usually available in variety stores before Easter.) Glue the halves together and decorate the egg in any number of ways – perhaps using a permanent marker to draw a face. When tipped it will right itself. A classic "folk art toy," this appeals to the younger toddlers and infants who are not yet walking. You could put a jingle bell inside for a sound effect...just be sure the egg is glued securely shut.

Rolling Noisy Barrel

Find a round cardboard or metal container with a top, such as an oatmeal box, a metal kitchen canister, or large coffee can. Put noisy junk inside such as jingle bells, jar lids, etc. Tape both ends on securely. Glue magazine pictures of objects the child will recognize on the outside of the barrel. Cover the whole thing with clear contact paper to protect the pictures. Let the child have fun rolling this noisy toy around the room.

Homemade Pull Toys

Sometimes people buy pull toys to encourage toddlers to walk. Toddlers don't need any encouragement to walk! However, a toddler will enjoy a good pull toy for the cause and effect response the toy gives. While there are many available to purchase, you can make your own versions. A short string tied to any variety of "junk objects" will give children something fun to drag around that makes noise when it moves. Keep safety in mind – no sharp edges, nothing small enough to swallow. (Never use as a crib toy.) Some possible things to use: jingle bells inside a metal can with the top glued on, a number of jar lids with a hole punched in the middle (file hole smooth), an aluminum pie tin, or several tied together.

Hanging Objects

Hang some interesting things from the ceiling with string. Possibilities are foam rubber balls, beach balls, or stuffed animals. Adjust the length of the string so that the objects hang above the level of the child's head but still within reach. Show the child how to hit the object with his hand to make it swing back and forth. You might try hanging several different objects at varying heights. While the toddler is having fun with the cause and effect he is also developing shoulder and torso muscles and developing balance. For variety, show the child how to bat at the objects with paper towel tubes.

Safety Note: Be careful that the strings aren't low enough to get around the children's necks. Hanging balloons is not a good idea because if they break children could choke on the balloon rubber.

Radio Play

An old radio is a wonderful play tool for toddlers. There are several ways the toddlers can practice cause and effect with a radio. They can turn it on and off. They can change the volume. And, of course, they can change the station. Do they learn to stop turning the knob when they get to a station? Do they move their bodies when they hear music? Do they react to speaking voices? Use a battery operated radio and make sure the cover to the battery compartment is secure.

FREQUENTLY ASKED QUESTIONS

Much of a certain child's "misbehavior" seems to be designed to "get a rise out of me." I feel like I'm a giant cause and effect toy. How should I handle it?

If possible, ignore the behavior so the child does not get the effect he is looking for. It will become uninteresting and the child will stop. However, if the behavior threatens to be destructive or hurtful, you cannot ignore it. If you feel a child is misbehaving to get your attention, try to provide extra attention when the child is being good. Also, provide many legitimate experiences for the child in which he can make things happen and feel his power.

CHAPTER 8

Making a **M**ark

A large piece of butcher paper has been taped down, covering a table top in a busy toddler classroom. Michael and Erica wander by, stop momentarily and pick up crayons that are attached to the table legs with long pieces of yarn. At the same time they scribble on the paper, making funny noises and giving each other eye contact. Just as quickly, they drop the crayons and are off to new adventures.

It is the cause and effect phenomenon that toddlers enjoy in doing art work – rather than the lofty notions of creativity or esthetics. "I do *this* – move my hand to the side – and *that* happens – there's a colorful streak on the paper."

Art activities for toddlers should be kept simple. Caregivers are often disappointed or frustrated because they spent far longer setting up the art activity than the toddlers spent doing it. They may be tempted to "doctor up" the child's creation so she will have something presentable to take home, a practice which is totally unacceptable!

Remember that it's the immediate cause and effect – a very momentary action – that appeals to toddlers. It is common for them to show no interest at all in the final product – or even not to recognize it at the end of the day. This does not mean that it is not worth doing! In the beginning the toddler pays very little attention to what she is doing. She may not even look at the paper. But as she gains experience, she notices the effect of actions and tries variations. These are the beginnings of eye-hand coordination needed later to learn to write. It is possible that the spark of aesthetic appreciation may be ignited then, also, but that is not the primary objective.

HINTS:

- Do with one child at a time or a very small group, not more than three.
- Have everything ready ahead of time.
- Have waterproof smocks for the children to wear.
- If they seem to have no idea of what to do with the material, you could either parallel play or specifically show them how to use materials, but not what to make.
- Stay close to observe, admire and enjoy.
- Provide the envelope of language.

FINGERPAINTING

Fingerpainting is the classical art activity for toddlers – and a very good place to start. They enjoy it as much for the feel as for the cause and effect designs they make. To introduce fingerpainting, simply sit down and do it yourself, describing what you are doing. Have the child ready to go at the same time so she can join right in. Don't draw anything – just mess around. "Oh look – there's a big blob of blue paint in front of me. I'm smearing it around and around. It feels good. Ooooh, pretty! Can you do that too?" A technique which is not recommended is to put your hands over the toddler's and guide her hands. Better to let the toddler approach the material on her own terms.

If you are in charge of a group of toddlers, don't attempt to have them all paint at once. Let two or three paint while the others continue to play at something else. Be sure to protect clothing with waterproof smocks and roll up sleeves. If you don't have a sink close by it's a good idea to have a bucket of soapy water and a sponge handy for quick cleanups.

Although it is common to use such things as pudding, whipped cream or yogurt for fingerpainting, with the reasoning that it won't hurt toddlers if they taste it, this is **not** a recommended practice. Toddlers would assume that food is there to eat. It's hard enough to get them not to smear their spaghetti sauce, and it could put you at cross purposes with parents. If you use non-toxic, safe ingredients, children will not be harmed by fingerpaint.

Paint on the Table Top

Allow children to fingerpaint directly on a table top. They can be free in their movements and unrestricted by the size of the paper. If you want to save the painting you can make a monoprint. Use any type of paper – inexpensive newsprint works fine. Press it over the child's painting on the table top and lift off carefully to reveal a print.

Fun Cleanup

To clean the fingerpaint off the top of a table top, give the child a paper or styrofoam cup and show her how to invert the cup and scrape it across the top of the table. The paint will pile up on the side of the cup and can be scraped off into a container. This makes interesting "roads" that the child can then play with. A squeegee is also fun for a child to use.

Paint on Cafeteria Trays

Give each child her own individual cafeteria tray to finger-paint on. These contain the mess and can be rinsed off in a sink when the child is finished. The child can do this, and might enjoy watching the color dilute as it mixes with water and goes down the drain.

Shaving Cream

Many toddlers will not like to get their hands messy with paint, but they will almost invariably love to fingerpaint with shaving cream. A soft, billowy, good smelling mound of shaving cream is almost irresistible. It has the advantages of being easy to clean up, and leaving everything, including the artists, cleaner and sweeter smelling than before. For variety you could add a few drops of food coloring to the shaving cream to create pretty pastels. Make sure to rinse their hands afterwards to avoid skin irritation.

Is it safe? Manufacturers of shaving cream say that once the shaving cream is out of the can it is basically soap. While a child will probably taste it – once – a child would have to eat a large amount of shaving cream to have stomach upset. The one caution about painting with shaving cream is that children might rub it in their eyes, so supervision is necessary.

Heated Shaving Cream

It's a wonderful treat, and very soothing, to fingerpaint with heated shaving cream. To heat the shaving cream you can simply place the can in hot water for a few minutes. (DO NOT MICROWAVE!)

Commercial and Homemade Fingerpaint

Commercial fingerpaint is wonderfully creamy and smells good. It is a lovely luxury, but there are many recipes for homemade fingerpaint that work very well. Commercial fingerpaint paper, likewise, is a nice luxury, but coated shelf paper works, if you feel a need to have the child take a product home. Here are some simple recipes for fingerpaint. Add food coloring or tempera paint for color.

Cornstarch-Water-Glycerine Fingerpaint

Mix 1/2 cup of cornstarch with 1/4 cup of cold water. Then gradually add 2 cups of hot water, stirring to prevent lumps. Cook over low heat until it begins to boil. Remove from heat and add another 1/2 cup of cold water and 1 tablespoon glycerine. The glycerine makes it slippery and slows up the drying process.

Cornstarch-Gelatin Fingerpaint

Mix 1/2 cup of cornstarch with 3/4 cup of cold water to a smooth paste in a saucepan. Soak 1 envelope of unflavored gelatin in 1/4 cup of water. Pour 2 cups of boiling water into the saucepan with the cornstarch mixture, stirring. Cook over medium heat, stirring, until it comes to a boil and is clear. Remove from heat and stir in gelatin.

Starch-Soap-Baby Powder Fingerpaint

Simply mix liquid laundry starch, soap flakes or powder and baby powder to a smooth consistency.

Change Textures

None of the above recipes are sacred. Fool around with them or make up your own recipes. Try adding textures to the paint by mixing in such things as coffee grounds, cornmeal, sawdust or Vaseline to vary the experience. Some people like to add fragrance with oil of wintergreen, perfume or cooking extracts. This certainly is pleasant, but it may make the children even more prone to eating the paint.

Window Painting

Toddlers love to fingerpaint on a low window. When the paint dries they can use their fingers or a cotton tipped swab to scribble designs through the paint. Mix dish detergent into the paint so it will wash off easily.

Mirror Painting

What fun to fingerpaint on a mirror and slowly cover up your reflection! Later the paint can be rubbed off little by little to reveal the image again. "Peek-a-Boo!"

Do a Group Fingerpainting

Tape a long piece of shelf paper to a table top and let several children paint at once. They'll enjoy the social aspect.

SCRIBBLING

Most toddlers really love to scribble. As any parent knows, if you give a child a crayon, and don't watch closely, there will be crayon marks on the walls and furniture. So, give toddlers plenty of legitimate opportunities to scribble on paper. If you vary the material you give them for scribbling, they will learn about different textures and colors. You may even notice differences in their scribbling style with different materials.

You will notice that a child's scribbling usually follows a predictable progression. The youngest child usually starts with a series of horizontal lines. Later vertical lines appear. Then, round and round, non-ending circles. Later you may notice a completed, closed circle. Almost all children make "spider" or "sun" patterns eventually with lines radiating out from a central circle. This does not usually appear until a child is well past three.

It really doesn't matter what kind of paper you use. Even newspaper is fine – children don't seem to mind the print at all. Shelf paper, newsprint, paper grocery sacks and butcher paper are all inexpensive or free and serve the purpose well.

Crayons

"Fat" crayons are good to use because they are easy to grip and they don't break easily.

Chunky Crayons

"Chunky" crayons are available commercially. They are shaped like hockey pucks and children grasp them with their whole hand. With these crayons children can use large sweeping arm movements on a large scribbling surface such as a piece of butcher paper taped to the floor. You can make these big crayons yourself. Do **not** do it with children around because the melting wax is dangerous. Peel the paper off old, broken crayons and sort them by color into individual compartments in an old muffin tin (sprayed with non-stick cooking spray). Children can do this part for you ahead of time. Put the muffin tin into a warm oven and check it every now and then. (For extra safety, place the muffin tin into a large pan of water in the oven.) As soon as the wax is melted, remove the muffin tin from the oven and allow it to cool completely. Then pop the chunky crayons out.

Felt-Tipped Marking Pens

The advantage of felt-tipped marking pens is that with very little pressure the child gets brilliant streaks of color. Make sure you get *water soluble* markers, not "permanent" markers.

The disadvantages of markers are:

• Unlike crayons, the amount of pressure a child exerts does not affect the quality of the mark.

• If the caps get lost the pens dry out and are useless.

• Children soon learn that markers, unlike crayons, color skin very well. Even water-soluble markers can be hard to wash off.

• Some toddlers like to suck on the end like a bottle, resulting in colored lips and teeth...therefore, supervise closely.

• The caps can pose a choking hazard. So mix up some plaster of Paris and pour it into an old baking pan. It should be the consistency of very thick cream when you pour it. (Don't pour excess down the drain!) Sink the marking pen tops, open side up, into the plaster halfway up to the open end. Let the plaster harden. Then put the marking pens into the caps like birthday candles. Since toddlers love to stick things in holes, you won't have any trouble getting them to put the markers away.

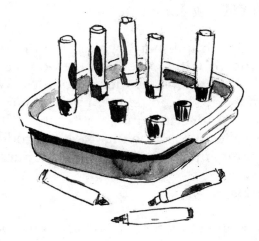

Chalk

With chalk children experience yet another texture. Colored construction paper is a good surface to scribble on. Chalkboards are fun for toddlers when they learn to make marks disappear with an eraser. And scribbling with large, chunky chalk on a sidewalk or concrete surface is great fun.

A Scribble Easel

Tape a large piece of paper to an easel. Tie a piece of yarn about two feet long around a fat crayon with a notch in it so the yarn doesn't slip off. Tie the other end to the top of the easel. This is now a "scribble place" where a child may make a mark whenever she pleases, without waiting for an adult to set out the materials. You could attach several different colors of crayons.

Paint In Roll-On Deodorant Bottles

By pressing your thumb hard against the plastic collar and prying underneath with something metal, you can pop the ball and collar off roll-on deodorant bottles. Wash out the inside and fill it with liquid tempera paint. Snap the ball and collar back on. You've just made a "giant ball point pen" that's a very effective scribbling tool for toddlers. Bright swatches of paint appear on the paper with minimal mess.

Other Materials

Let toddlers scribble with pencils, ball point pens, colored pencils, and other drawing materials from time to time. Variety keeps it interesting.

BRUSH PAINTING

Brush painting is messy and requires close supervision, but is very enjoyable to older toddlers and two-year-olds and worth the effort.

To minimize the mess:

- Protect children's clothing with waterproof smocks. Be sure to roll up sleeves.

- Protect the floor with newspapers, a large piece of vinyl, or perhaps an old shower curtain.

- If you're using an easel you may want to cover it with aluminum foil, newspaper or contact paper.

To keep paint jars from tipping over, pour small amounts of paint (1/2" or so) in plastic yogurt cups. Cut holes in sponges exactly the same size as the cup bottoms and sink the cup into the hole. The sponge will catch the drips, greatly reducing the mess.

What Kind of Paint to Use

Water

Plain water is a good way to start. Toddlers seem to enjoy it as much as paint. They learn how brushes work and you can attempt to show them how to wipe the brush on the side of the can. Painting the sidewalk or the outside of the building on a hot sunny day with water is an activity toddlers love. It's fun to see the surface get dark where it is wet and slowly fade as it dries.

Liquid Tempera

This can be purchased in little bottles (poster paints) but is quite expensive in that form. School supply stores and catalogs sell liquid tempera by the pint, quart or gallon. It's mixed just right and is a good consistency.

Powdered Tempera

Powdered tempera is less expensive than liquid tempera but it can be a bother to mix. The water does not absorb right away. Mix two parts water with one part powdered paint in a jar. Don't shake it, just allow it to sit and the water will gradually absorb into the paint. When it is all absorbed, stir it a bit with a stick. Prepare the day before you plan to use it.

Add Variety

Try mixing paint in varying thicknesses. Many people use liquid starch as a paint extender. Make the paint thick and gloppy one day, thin and runny another time. Vary the texture and color of the paint. Offer different colors from time to time. Mix things in with the paint such as soapflakes, salt, coffee grounds, or baby powder for a different effect.

Brushes

Standard long-handled easel brushes are too hard for toddlers and two-year-olds to manipulate. Often you end up with paint dripping down the elbow and drops of paint flung all over the place. Instead, buy some 2" brushes with 6" handles at the hardware store. Put one brush in each jar of paint you offer the toddler. Young children seem to be able to handle this size of brush quite well. But also look for all kinds of different brushes children can experiment with.

Brush Variations:

- sponge tipped paint trimming tools
- small sponge rollers
- small pieces of sponge clipped on the end of a spring-type clothespin.
- sponges without handles
- cotton-tipped swabs
- feathers
- old toothbrushes
- combs

Easels

The advantage of an easel is that it presents the painting surface vertically – the child can see the whole thing easily and his arm does not drag across the paint. Although they're nice to have, it is certainly not necessary to have an easel for a child to enjoy painting. If you do use an easel, make sure it is not too high. The paper should be at the child's eye level.

Homemade Table Top Easel

Make a simple cardboard easel by removing one side of a cardboard grocery carton and taping the remaining open edges together so that it forms a triangular tube. This can be taped to the table at the back so it does not slide away when the child exerts pressure with the brush. Tape the paper to the front or hold it in place with clamps or spring-type clothespins attached to the sides.

Attach Paper Directly to a Protected Wall

Open out a large cardboard box such as an appliance shipping carton. Nail or tape a large section of this to the wall. You can then tape painting paper directly to this. You need a little table close by to put the paint cups on. You could protect the wall in other ways, such as hanging vinyl over the wall or putting contact paper over the wall.

Fence Painting

Attach paper to a fence outside. No worry about drips!

Mirrors

Paint on mirrors. It's great fun to slowly cover up your image with paint.

Plexiglass and Windows

Use one of the new plexiglass easels or put children on opposite sides of a low window and let them paint on both sides of it at the same time. Great fun because they can see each other through it and notice marks being made by the other in relation to marks they are making themselves.

OTHER PROCESSES

Sand Painting

Sand can be colored by "washing" it with food coloring and letting the water evaporate. Some caregivers just mix sand with powdered tempera paint. Then put the colored sand in spice bottles with shaker tops. Have the child dribble glue onto paper from a squeeze bottle, or brush it on from a small amount you have poured into a small container. Or, allow the child to "fingerpaint" with paste on paper. Let the child shake the colored sand over it, then tip the paper to let the excess fall off. Other types of materials to shake onto glue or paste: colored salt, sugar sprinkles, cornmeal, baby powder.

Safety Note: Do **not** use glitter, because it can cause damage if children rub it in their eyes.

There are a couple problems with this type of activity. Some adults are too limiting. They feel glue is too expensive to allow the child to use it freely so they put the glue on the paper for the child. Or the adult feels it's necessary to do the sand shaking, so it's not so messy. These adult actions rob the child of the value of the activity, putting the toddler into the role of a passive observer. Put the paper the child is using in a cafeteria tray so that the excess sand can be tipped right into the tray. You could also do this outside at a small table set up right over the sand box.

Tearing Paper

Get several old magazines or newspapers and tell a small group of children, "These are old and we don't need them any more. Let's tear them up." The sound of several people tearing paper at once is fun to hear in itself and toddlers like the sensation of using both their hands in opposition to each other. Later they can paste their torn pieces to another sheet of paper.

Pasting

Pasting can be an enjoyable experience for toddlers if you are not too concerned with an acceptable looking final product. You might start by letting the toddler tear colored paper scraps into small pieces.

Often young children are most interested in fingerpainting with the paste. Some may not enjoy the sticky feeling on their fingers; others will be fascinated by it, spending most of the time looking at their fingers sticking to each other, and seeing how paper scraps stick to their finger tips. If they do get a scrap of paper to the page, they then pound on it with their hand to make it stick and sometimes they get frustrated when the paper scrap sticks to their hand instead of the paper. Sometimes adults give children pictures or cut up greeting cards to paste and are frustrated when children put the paste on the front of the card rather than on the back.

Pasting is really a fairly complex process. If you approach it as a good "messing around" experience and generally leave the children alone, it will have value. It loses value when the teacher takes over and does part or most of the project.

Gluing

Like pasting, gluing is a complex project requiring several steps, and learning to put the glue on the back side of the thing to be stuck down. The act of making something stick on is not a satisfying visible effect – they can't *see* the glue or understand why it happens. So what do they typically do when offered this activity? They dribble the glue, being much more interested in watching the glue come out of the bottle than in what it does on the paper. Instead, let them do salt dribbles.

However, again, if you regard this as a good "messing around" activity, children can enjoy it and gain experience with the material. If you're concerned about children wasting glue, you could transfer white glue from a large bottle into very small bottles for children to use. Some caregivers have had limited success in putting the glue in small cups, jar lids, or bottle tops, giving the children craft sticks or cotton tipped swab applicators to use with it. Remember, resist the temptation to put the glue on the paper for the child because then the value of the activity is lost.

Salt Dribbles

Mix equal parts of flour, salt and water and add liquid paint for color. Pour into plastic squeeze bottles. Then let children squeeze this out in dribbles onto pieces of cardboard or plastic coffee can lids. Put the the dribble paintings up to dry for a day if you want to preserve the product for parents. Offer several colors. Toddlers love to use the squeeze bottles for anything – but here it's legitimate! The colors pool together without mixing, making interesting patterns, and toddlers love to watch the mixture come out of the bottle. Squeezing the bottles gives their hand muscles some practice and strength building exercise. The surprise is that although this paint is creamy when it comes out of the squeeze bottle, it dries sparkly because of the salt.

Print Making

Potato printing, gadget printing, sponge printing, wonderful projects for children three years old and older, are usually not satisfying for toddlers. They usually "paint" with the objects rather than printing with them. They move their hand to see the swatch of color – the immediate effect...so why not just let them paint?

In all fairness, some caregivers of two-year-olds have, with patience, been able to teach the children to do the printing process successfully. You can make a simple print pad by saturating some sponge cloth with paint and laying it in a shallow tray. The child can then press the object onto the sponge and then the paper. The child will enjoy pounding something up and down and seeing the repeated pattern. Another variation is to let them hold an object such as a cookie cutter and pound it repeatedly onto a slab of play dough.

Art Techniques Not Recommended for Toddlers

- **Watercolor trays.** Paint trays with the little solid pans of color that you can buy in most variety stores are not good to use with toddlers. The process is too complex. The child must get the brush wet in water, swirl it around on the solid paint to get the color on the brush, make the mark (often the brush is too fragile for a toddler's heavy hand) and rinse the brush before starting the process all over for a second color. You end up with a ruined tray of paints. Reserve water color trays for older children.

- **Cutting.** Toddlers do not have the coordination in their hands to use scissors effectively. Instead, allow them the pleasure of tearing paper. To give the child practice in using those muscles of his hand, you could let the child cut coils of play dough with blunt-end scissors. This activity will occupy some toddlers for a long time. Supervise close-ly…even though the child will not be successful at cutting paper, hair seems amazingly easy for toddlers to cut!

Some Things to Do with Toddler Art Work

Remember the principle that with toddler art work it's the process, not the final product that is important to the child. For this reason, it's probably okay if you do nothing at all with the art work. Many caregivers, however, feel a need to display art work to show parents that it is taking place and parents like to show their children that they value their creative efforts.

- The refrigerator is really a good place for children's art work at home. You can attach the works easily with magnets and because it's right in the center of things it will give the work importance.

- Frame it. Find an old picture frame or make one out of burlap or calico or mat board. Then you can change the picture in this frame every few days or so.

- Paintings can be made into greeting cards. Cut them into rectangles (with the child's permission) and glue these onto the front of a folded white piece of paper to make a card.

- Paintings and scribbles can also be made into wrapping paper, book covers, box covers, etc.

- A portfolio/scrapbook. Of course, you won't want to save every single thing, but it's nice to save representative samples and date them. You'll be amazed at how you can trace a child's development through her art work.

- Use the back of paintings or drawings to write a child-dictated letter to grandparents or special friends.

- Thematic decor. Many caregivers like to decorate their room with seasonal or thematic art work done by children. They accomplish this with toddlers by precutting the paper the child is to paint on into shapes such as pumpkins or teddy bears. If you try to get toddlers to make a particular thing such as a Santa or a flower, you are destined for failure. But when you give children precut shapes on which to paint or scribble, they can paint freely and gain experience with new types of boundaries. You are gradually increasing their awareness of shapes.

FREQUENTLY ASKED QUESTIONS

What do you say to the child?

If you feel you must comment on a child's scribbling, or if a child proudly shows you her art work, you can say something like, "Wow...you made lots and lots of blue marks! They go round and round and round." Don't ask the child what it is supposed to be. At this age they honestly don't have anything in mind. They enjoy making marks for their own sake. Purists!

What do you tell the parents?

Simply explain the value that children got from the "messing around" activity – gradually learning eye-hand coordination, learning about the properties of different materials, enjoying the social interaction with other children. Explain that learning to be creative comes from many experiences with a wide variety of materials, and lots of other activities letting the children know that they have interesting ideas.

CHAPTER 9

Poking, Fitting, Stacking, Dumping

*T*ed, with the respon-
sibility of babysitting his
two-and-one-half-year-old
niece, Cindy, got a call from his
ice fishing buddies. The conditions were perfect...come out to
the lake. Not wanting to miss
out, he decided to take Cindy
along. What could happen?
While he had his back turned
and was talking to his buddies,
Cindy was playing quietly,
dropping 47 of his expensive fishing lures through the hole in the ice
and watching them glitter as they floated to the bottom of the lake.

Poking Things In Holes

Show any toddler a surface with holes in it and he will immediately stick a finger in the hole! This compulsion probably
has something to do with "object permanence" – learning
that something continues to exist even if one can't see it.
There may also be some fascination with their developing
eye-hand coordination – that they can make something go
exactly where they want it to go, and fitting things together.
There are many good commercial toys that allow toddlers to
practice this interest. School supply companies carry large

rubber pegboards with either 25 or 100 holes in them and large, brightly colored plastic pegs to go with them. This toy gets good concentration from toddlers as they practice eye-hand coordination. There are also other toys that involve putting wooden cylinders into holes. Shape sorting boxes are good for this purpose. The popular Snap-Lock beads by Fisher-Price or Giant Legos and similar toys involve sticking something in a hole. Toddlers also like to put their fingers into these holes.

With toys that have pieces, make sure the pieces are not small enough for toddlers to choke on or shove into their ears or nostrils (the ever-present, most convenient holes!). For this reason, many fine toys for preschoolers such as small wooden pegs, small beads, small fit-together toys, etc., **are not safe** to use with toddlers.

HOLES

Ball Through a Tube

A tennis ball and a large cardboard giftwrap tube or a mailing tube work well for this. For a more permanent version, you could use PVC pipe. Toddlers love to stick the ball in one end and see it come shooting out the other end. Attach the tube to a stair railing or to a fence outside with a basket to receive the balls at the end. You can vary what you give the child to put through the tube from day to day.

Shape Sorting Boxes

These are very popular commercial toys marketed to parents of toddlers. They are often a bit difficult for young toddlers. Make an easier version yourself by cutting a round hole in a plastic coffee can lid or a shoebox lid. Let the child drop small toys and objects through the hole.

Plunker

Cut an X in the plastic lid of a coffee can or margarine tub. Let the child push wooden beads, napkin rings or other objects through the X. They will love the plunking noise it makes.

Color Sorter Plunker

You could make a color sorter by spray painting several coffee cans different colors or covering them with colored self-adhesive paper. Then tell the child to put the things that are the same color as this in the can. They may not get the idea because "color" is an abstract concept – so don't get frustrated. Your pet puppet could help.

Slot Boxes for Cleanup

Use a "boutique" type tissue box for crayon storage. Toddlers love to drop the crayons through the slot to put them away and reach in to get another.

You could use cardboard boxes to store toys that have many pieces. Cut a hole in the lid of the box and children are much more likely to cooperate and help clean up by putting the pieces through the hole. Provide a different box for each toy.

Sticking Straws Through Peg Board Holes

Plastic drinking straws fit through the holes of the pegboard backs on classroom furniture. Let children stick the straw from the back of a shelf unit into one of the compartments.

Stringing Beads

To toddlers, the appeal of stringing beads is actually that of poking something through a hole. The traditional beads and laces you can buy are often too difficult for two-year-olds because the laces are soft and floppy. Large, brightly colored wooden beads are a good size for twos to handle. Use thin plastic tubing (like aquarium tubing) instead of the laces that come with the beads, and two-year-olds will find more success. Find other things that are fun to string – everything from thread spools, to hair curlers, to napkin rings. The world is full of interesting things with holes. Later, children will enjoy stringing O-shaped cereal onto shoelaces.

Stacking Rings

This is another popular commercial toy for toddlers. Infants and toddlers usually pay little attention to the relative size of the rings, nor will they always put them on in order. The appeal is putting the stick through the hole in the ring. Here are some homemade variations:

- Large wooden curtain rings can be placed over a stick.
- Rubber canning rings can be fit over a can or cardboard cylinder attached to a base.
- Anchor a thick wooden dowel in play dough and let the children thread napkin rings of all types over the end.

Compartment Boxes

Retail beverage stores will probably be able to give you boxes that have individual compartments for bottles. Collect some empty one-litre bottles. Let the child put the tubes or bottles into the compartments. They also like to put toys, animals, etc., in the compartments. Attach a small rope to the box and the toddler can give them a ride, dragging them around the room.

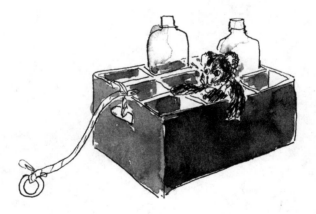

Fitting Things Together

This is a refinement of sticking things through holes. Toddlers like to put things inside of other things, match objects to holes, and make things stick. Commercial toys such as plastic blocks that fit together (make sure you get the kind that are too big for a child to choke on), nesting and stacking cups, and toys with small indentations in which to fit smaller items such as small wooden people appeal to toddlers for this reason.

EMPTYING AND FILLING

One way to occupy a toddler is to give him a container of some sort with some objects in it (doesn't much matter what, as long as it's safe) and let him dump it out and refill it again and again. You probably won't even have to say much in the way of an introduction...the toddler will do it naturally. There are many variations to this theme which will maintain the child's interest. In the process, the child is developing coordination of hand and arm muscles. The magic of gravity accompanied by satisfying *cause and effect* noises compound the interest.

Fill and Spill Bucket

Suspend a small bucket from the ceiling so it hangs about a foot above the floor. Place a plastic dishpan under it. Put a bunch of small toys in the dishpan. Show the toddler how to put the toys from the dishpan into the bucket, and then dump them back into the dishpan. Toddlers like to do this over and over again.

Toy Transfer Game

Put two dishpans on opposite sides of the room. Fill one with small toys. Provide a container with a handle that is fun to carry such as a colorful basket. Show the child how to load the toys into the basket, carry them across the room and dump them into the empty dishpan. Then, of course, the child can transfer the toys back into another container with a handle, and bring them back to the first dishpan across the room. As the child enjoys this activity over and over, you can talk about concepts of "empty and full."

Little Play People and an Egg Carton

The child will enjoy putting one play person, or some other toy in each space of an egg carton. You could tie a piece of yarn to one end and make it into a pull toy. Tie several together and make a train!

Sand and Water Play

Filling and pouring are, of course, major concentrations in sand and water play. Just concentrate on giving the toddler a wide variety of containers to use over time. Spray can tops give you much variety in size and color and are fun to use.

Puppet Game with a Box of Junk

Since a toddler will do almost anything for a puppet, you can use your puppet to help the child empty or fill a container and talk about what is happening. The puppet may ask the child to find some specific things in the room to put in the container. This is a very effective tool if you want the toddler's help in cleaning up.

Travel Kit Toys

Travel kits with plastic containers for soap, toothbrush and creams make a great toy for a toddler because it provides things that need different hand motions to open and close them. When the child gets bored with using it just as it is putting empty containers in  and out of the larger zippered compartment, try filling the containers with things that match their shape. This will give the toddler an added challenge. Playing cards could go in the soap box. Straws and popsicle sticks could go in the toothbrush holder. Jar lids could go in the plastic jars. The zippered travel case is itself a valuable container for the above treasures, and the child will like to zip and unzip it.

FREQUENTLY ASKED QUESTIONS

Why should we bother finding toys and activities involving holes? What are they getting out of it?

There are many possible benefits. You are providing "re-direction" – allowing a way that's okay to practice something that toddlers do compulsively. They are also learning cognitive concepts of size, shape and position. The fine motor coordination involved relates to other skills learned later, such as holding a pencil or buttoning.

CHAPTER 10

Splashing and Playing with Water

*Y*ou go outside after a rainstorm and before you can make a quick grab your toddler heads straight for the mud puddle. Usually he beats you there! Any type of water play is an excellent cause and effect activity, and endlessly fascinating to toddlers. Mothers have known this ever since the bathtub was invented. "When all else fails, put them in the tub." Playing with water is as close to a "compulsion" as anything you could think of with toddlers, so you might as well make it legitimate and gear up for it.

The reason water play holds the attention of toddlers so well is because it produces such a wide variety of responses. Some things bob up to the surface when you release them under water. Some things sink to the bottom when you do the same thing. What wonderful noises water makes!

The youngest toddlers will enjoy just splashing the water and watching it dribble off a washcloth. They are enjoying the feel and sound of water. As children get older they will become more and more interested in "doing things" with water. Possibilities are endless – but here are some favorites for starters.

WATER PLAY

Sponges

What a great invention the sponge is! A package of inexpensive sponges will find many uses around toddlers besides cleaning.

When using sponges with water play, children will discover many entertaining uses. Squeeze them out and they float. You can make them into little rafts and give rides to little wooden people, plastic animals, etc. You can blow them to make them move.

The "mechanics" of sponges will interest children and allowing them plenty of time to just play is the best way to let them learn. Later you can offer a challenge: "Can you fill this little bowl just using the sponge?"

Washing Rocks

Two-year-olds really like rocks. Give them small sponges and some rocks and invite them to wash the rocks. They will discover that rocks change color when they are wet, and slowly fade back as they dry. This is a nice activity to do outside on a warm day.

Pouring

A collection of containers of different sizes and shapes and a tub of water are all you need here. Margarine tubs, cut off plastic bleach bottles, plastic milk jugs, film canisters, coffee scoops, spray can tops, plastic bottles and jars are all possibilities. A small funnel would be a nice addition. Don't present too many at one time. Two or three containers is enough at first. Later you can ask, "What things would you like to pour with today?" and allow the child to choose. Pouring is a good way to develop eye-hand coordination.

Dribbles

Poke holes in the bottom of a margarine tub and children will enjoy filling it with water, lifting it, and watching the water dribble out.

Basting

A large meat baster will attract the concentration of toddlers. When you first introduce this to the child it is a good idea to have two – one for yourself and one for the child. "Look what I can do with mine. I squeeze this and bubbles come out. Then the water goes in. Can you do that with yours? Now when I squeeze it I can make the water go in this jar... watch." Show the child how to empty one container of water and fill another using the baster. After she has had a chance to play with it freely for a while, you could have her transfer colored water from one margarine tub to another. Small molded plastic pet food dishes with two compartments work well for this. A baking pan underneath could catch drips.

Plastic Eye Droppers

These, of course, operate from the same principle as meat basters, but on a smaller scale. Instead of using the whole hand to squeeze, the older child uses just the forefinger and thumb. They can transfer water back and forth between small containers or onto sponges.

Ice Cube Tray Color Transfers

Two-year-olds will enjoy transferring colored water in an ice cube tray. Partially fill a white ice cube tray with clear water. Put a few drops of food coloring in one compartment. Put a second color in a second compartment at the other end. The child can transfer the color from one compartment to another using the eye dropper, and will pick up some information about color mixing. If you add a third color – red, blue and yellow – the child will end up with all the colors of the rainbow. Finally, she may enjoy dropping these pretty colors onto white paper towels or coffee filters with the eye dropper to make pretty color blotches.

Squeeze Bottles

Save the empty plastic squeeze bottles that dish detergent, and such things as catsup, mustard, glue and shampoo come in. Especially good are the clear plastic bottles. This allows children to see what's going on inside the bottle as well as the squirt. Children enjoy watching the bubbles come out when they squeeze the bottle under water. Toddlers like to hold bottles upside down and watch the water dribble out. Once the toddler has had plenty of time to play with a squeeze bottle, challenge her to fill another plastic bottle with a small opening.

Running Water

Faucets and drinking fountains fascinate toddlers because they get the added cause and effect action of turning them on and off. And you can do so much with the running stream of water that comes out of a garden hose! Give a two-year-old a garden hose to fill a wading pool and she'll be occupied for a long time – and the pool will not necessarily become full. If you're adventurous and don't mind getting wet on a hot day, show your two-year-old how to work the nozzle on a garden hose!

WASHING THINGS

Very popular activities, all of these. To the fascination of water play you're adding a new interest of two-year-olds – dramatic play – acting like a grown-up. When water play merges into dramatic play it takes on another dimension. The combination can't be beat to hold their interest.

Wash Dolls

When you give a toddler a doll to bathe, have clothes on the doll and see if the toddler will think to take them off. (Children will usually be able to undress a doll long before they can dress it.) The more real "props" you can provide, the better. A small bar of soap, a washcloth and towel, a comb will do the trick. It might be fun to put a tape recorder near-by and record what the child says to the doll.

Wash Doll Clothes

Provide soapy water – and perhaps some rinse water. Show the child how to wring out wet things. It will add extra fun for two-year-olds if you can rig up a low clothesline and add some clothespins.

Wash Dishes

A real dish drainer, a dish tub, plastic dishes, a dish rag and warm soapy water will get amazingly accurate imitations from your toddler...provided she has actually seen someone washing dishes!

Wash the Car

Outside on a warm day toddlers will enjoy washing their riding toys or small cars and trucks, or helping someone wash a real car.

BUBBLES!

Blow Bubbles Through a Straw

Once they get the hang of it, two-year-olds love to blow through a straw into a bowl of soapy water to make a frothy mass of bubbles. What a delightful effect for their efforts! A great sound too! Let children practice with plain, non-soapy water first to learn how to blow out rather than suck in. (Of course, give each child her own straw.)

Chasing Bubbles

You don't need to purchase commercial bubble soap. Just mix about two tablespoons of dishwashing liquid to a cup of water. A loop made from a pipe cleaner, finger holes in blunt scissors, etc., make fine bubble blowers. Your toddler will love chasing after and catching the bubbles you blow, or watching them float away in the breeze outside. Each breath brings a surprise! Try waving a plastic strawberry basket or cherry tomato basket dipped in bubble soap and see what happens!

Indoors, it's wonderful fun to plug in an electric fan (placed at least three feet from where children could get at it) and place the loaded bubble blower in front of it. The fan will blow the bubbles all over the room, to the delight of the children. You will, of course, supervise this closely, not letting children put their fingers near the fan. Put the fan away as soon as you are finished with the activity.

FREQUENTLY ASKED QUESTIONS

How can I minimize children geting wet?

Waterproof smocks are available from child care equipment suppliers and are a good idea. The constant reminder, "Keep the water in the tub (or water table)," will help somewhat. Show the child how to hold the containers over the center of the table. Stay fairly close by to calm children down if the play starts to get too exuberant. "This water is for pouring, not for splashing." Notice when they're doing it right: "You're doing a really good job keeping the water in the water table today!"

The floor can get wet and slippery; what can we do?

Again, the reminder, "Keep the water in the water table (or dish tub)," will help. Place the water table over a tiled area of the room. You might even choose to protect the floor with an old shower curtain or large, heavy piece of vinyl or vinyl floor runners. If you cut down the handle of either a string mop or sponge mop, children will greatly enjoy helping mop up. Another way to catch drips is to put dish tubs inside a small child's wading pool on a low table or on the floor. Spills land in the wading pool rather than on the floor. Or, put the whole water table inside a large wading pool.

The above two problems make water play an ideal outdoor activity in warm weather.

How can I prevent children drinking the water or sucking on bottles or basters?

It's inevitable that children will taste the water. This is one reason why it's important to use clean water each time. Do not let water sit overnight. Showing them what to do with the materials will help alleviate this. When they know other interesting things to do with bottles and basters they will be less likely just to suck on them. Supervise.

Children sometimes squirt each other with bottles or basters.

Say, "These bottles aren't for squirting people – they're for filling and emptying and squirting the water into these things." If the child persists, get her involved in something else.

Why do children sometimes seem overwhelmed?

A common error is to have too many things for the child to play with. You have to leave room for the water! If you have too many toys, the child will be too easily distracted and will not be able to play constructively. Better to offer a few well-chosen items and store the rest. Vary them from day to day.

CHAPTER 11

Touching, Tasting, Smelling, Looking — Sensory Play

G ive a young toddler a new, unfamiliar object and watch what happens. The object will go to the mouth immediately. "How does it taste?" "How does it feel?" "Does it have a smell?" Then the object will be turned over so all sides can be examined. Next he will probably shake it and hit it against the table or the floor to see what kind of sound it makes.

Toddlers vigorously use all of their senses to explore everything. One of the joys of working with children of this age is that the whole world is fresh and new to them. They are busily "gathering data." As they use all of their senses they gather information and gradually absorb concepts such as hot, soft, wet, salty, etc.

SOFTNESS

Most homes are full of soft things, but this is not always true of group care environments. It is important to have softness in a toddler's environment...things that give to the touch. It makes group care less "institutional" and more home-like, and it's pleasing to the senses. The most important soft thing in the room, of course, is a nice, soft adult with a frequently available lap. Other things that qualify are: pillows and cushions, soft chairs, stuffed animals, soft toys, yarn balls, grass, plants, sand, water, blankets, play dough, carpeting, draperies...what else can you think of? The whole idea is to create an atmosphere that is cozy and comfortable.

TEXTURES

The whole world is made up of textures. Toddlers want to experience all of them. Be conscious of this as children play. A nature walk or even ten minutes in the yard will offer many textures for the toddler to experience. See if you can let your fingers experience the world of textures the way a toddler's would.

Texture Board or Box

Glue variously textured materials to a large piece of cardboard, or all sides of a sturdy box, for children to feel. Place this where children can reach it. Usually they can be taught not to tear it apart if a teacher introduces it to a few children at a time and explains what it is for and how to use it, and children see the teacher repair it if it does get damaged. Possible textured materials to glue on: fake fur, cotton balls, aluminum foil, chamois, foam rubber, netting, sandpaper, velour, burlap, etc.

Texture Cards

Glue textured materials onto heavy cardboard cards. If you make two cards of each texture you can eventually ask a toddler if he can find the card that feels the *same*. Talk about what the child is touching.

Texture Book

Punch holes in heavy cardboard "pages" and put them in a looseleaf binder. Glue a different texture to each page. The stiffness of the pages makes this a better type of book than a cloth book with soft pages. The pages are easier for toddlers to turn.

Texture Snake

Sew variously textured material scraps together to make a

long tube. Use the toe of a sock for the head and sew on features. Stuff it with polyester stuffing material, old stockings, or other stuffing material. A very long snake can be a lot of fun to play with. You could use free out-of-date upholstery or drapery samples from a decorating store.

Texture Egg Carton

Glue small patches of different textures in the bottoms of egg carton compartments. The child will have to reach in with a pointed finger to feel the texture.

Texture Shelf or Table

Place interestingly-textured things on a shelf or table for children to pick up and feel and carry around. Possibilities: large bones, a chamois, a natural sponge, a large feather (washed), a ball of foil. Change these things frequently. Let children discover them and then use the "envelope of language" to talk about the textures with them.

Elephant Feely Box

Cut a hole about 4" in diameter in a large cardboard box and staple the sleeve of an old sweatshirt around it, shoulder end at the hole. Paint an elephant face on the box around the "trunk" and attach felt ears to the side of the box. Put things inside the box from the back and let the child  reach in through the trunk and guess what it is that he is feeling. (Of course, a plain box or bag would work too. This just adds an extra element of fun.)

Surprise Bag

It is fun to have a gaudy cloth bag (although any bag or even a sock will do) and call it your "Surprise Bag." (*Surprise* is one of a toddler's favorite words.) Put various things inside the bag and let the children feel the outside of the bag to guess what it is. Then let the child reach in and feel it. Finally, let him take out the "surprise."

Choose the Right Objects

As children approach three and have had a lot of experience with the "surprise bag" activity described above, you might try this variation. Put three or four familiar objects in the bag. Have the child put his hand inside the bag and you name the object for him to identify and pull out.

Or...find pairs of objects. Put one of each pair inside the bag. Then point to the visible object and see if the child can pull the same object out of the bag without looking.

Sticky Pictures

Cut a large square of self-adhesive paper and tape it low on the wall, sticky side out. Put a box of light-weight things to stick onto it close by. Possibilities: natural materials such as grass clippings, dried weeds, leaves, feathers, yarn, small fabric pieces, small pieces of paper. The toddler will be fascinated by feeling the sticky surface, saying "S-t-i-c-k-y," and pressing things onto it.

Sticky Tape

Is lunch late? Do you need to occupy children for a few minutes while you talk to someone? Just tear off small pieces of masking tape and give them to children. It's a good idea to do this routinely at the busy time right after lunch when children are being changed and you are setting out cots for nap time. Children enjoy the stickiness and the magic of the way it stays in place.

Tape Play

As long as you don't expect success or a final product, children can have lots of fun playing with all different kinds of tape. Make a collection. Cut off small pieces for them and stick them to the edge of a table. Give them different things to tape together, such as old greeting cards and paper scraps.

Stickers

Most children will do almost anything for a sticker, even if it comes off a banana. You can make your own stickers by cutting patterned self-adhesive paper into small pieces and peeling off the backs. They will enjoy sticking these to their skin, peeling them off and sticking them in other places. This fascination is probably one reason why children are so impressed by band-aids. (A box of band-aids is a wonderful birthday present for a toddler. They love the box too!)

TEMPERATURE

Everyday Hot and Cold

Everyday living gives children many first-hand experiences with the concepts of hot and cold. If you talk about it when opportunities present themselves vocabulary will be strengthened. "Be careful – the soup is hot." "The sun feels warm on my cheeks." "I'm putting ice in the drink to keep it cold."

Warm and Cold Rocks

Collect some nice, smooth rocks – perhaps about ten of them. Put half in the freezer and heat the others in hot water. Then put all the rocks on a table. Let the children feel the rocks and tell you if they're warm or cold. (Rocks retain heat and cold quite a long time.) Some two-year-olds may be able to sort them into two piles.

As a variation, do the same thing when you're outside with the child on a hot, sunny day. Let the child feel stones sitting out in the sun and compare them with stones that were buried or in the shade. They could even feel and compare the top side and the under side of a rock, or sunny and shady parts of the sidewalk.

More Warm and Cold Play Ideas

- Using the recipe on page 151 for cooked play dough, let children play with it while it is still warm. Feels good!

- Put snow in the water table or dish pan indoors.

- Float some ice cubes in the water table or a dish pan.

- Fill two zip lock bags with pudding – one with warm pudding, one with cold pudding. The child can play with these and hold them to his cheeks.

- Fill one dish pan with cold water, and one with warm water and let the child play with both side by side.

- Let the children feel the warm air coming from a hair dryer. Direct the air to different parts of a child's body. (Do **not** leave the hair dryer out for him to play with.)

SAND PLAY

Can you remember the pleasure you got from playing in sand as a child? Almost all toddlers enjoy digging. On the purely tactile level, children enjoy the feel of sand sifting through their fingers, and digging down, feeling the coolness of the buried sand contrasted with the warmth of the surface sand. Sand play can be a soothing, calming, absorbing activity for toddlers.

Much spontaneous learning takes place in the sandbox. Children become aware of the concepts of warm and cool, fine and coarse, dry and damp, empty and full. You have to "feed the muscles of imagination" in order for it to grow. Playing with mud, sand and water provides sensory input which is stored in the brain's "experience bank" to be used later in life.

Sandboxes

Sandboxes do not have to be elaborate. The main reason to have boundaries on a "box" is to keep the sand from spreading all over the yard. Untreated railroad ties or logs enclosing a space work well. Large truck or airplane tires, if you can get them, are also popular. Get a sturdy, secure cover to protect the sandbox from cats and other small animals when not in use. Anchor it down with rocks or other heavy objects. Check your local child care licensing regulations for any special guidelines regarding sand in the outdoor environment.

Type of Sand

The sand used for mixing cement – a fairly coarse sand – is good to use in sandboxes. Beach sand is generally too fine, it doesn't mold well, and it really clings to clothing.

Sand Toys

- A spoon or shovel and a small pail will happily occupy toddlers.

- Margarine tubs, bleach bottles with the tops cut off, spray can tops, coffee scoops and other "good junk" work just as well as purchased sand toys.

- A sifter is nice to have.

- Children will also enjoy poking twigs upright into the sand and drawing lines with sticks.

- Plastic or wooden animals and people are fun.

- They also love pushing small cars and trucks. Keep these just for the sandbox.

- Old plastic or metal dishes and other cooking stuff, even a small hibachi grill.

Sandbox Cheer

One caregiver who is a former cheerleader made up this cheer for children to do after playing in the sandbox, before going inside:

Clap your hands,
Stamp your feet,
(Child's name or group name) can't be beat!

Wipe your knees,
Rest awhile,
(Child's name) makes me smile!

Clap your hands,
Jump up and down,
(Child's name) is the best kid in town!

Wet Sand

If you can tolerate the mess and the weather is warm, adding a bucket of water to your sandbox will greatly enrich the sand play.

- Water changes the quality of the sand. It molds easily, and tracks and marks stay there.

- You can also supply water in a spray bottle for children to use, although this might be a bit hard for toddlers to manipulate.

- When water on sand forms strange shapes and designs, children notice patterns and make associations.

- They use the material in new ways to create new effects such as dribbling it in one spot to make a mountain.

- Children often draw pictures or create designs in wet sand.

- Wet sand lends itself readily to dramatic play. It becomes chocolate cake batter, coffee, pudding, etc., as children pour it into old dishes and pans. This inevitably leads children to acting out the various family roles in a new setting.

Sand Play Indoors

Sand can be put in a sensory table, or in dish pans indoors. If you are using dish pans, you can minimize the mess by placing the dish pans inside a child's wading pool on the table. Children will enjoy making roads and pouring almost as much as when playing outside. You can add water to the sand with less mess than if children were sitting in the sand outside. Having a child-sized broom and dust pan nearby will encourage the child's participation in the cleanup process.

Other Materials to Substitute for Sand

Other pourable substances are sometimes substituted for sand for indoor play, such as rice, cornmeal, birdseed, oatmeal. Each material offers a slightly different experience. Do not use beans because of toddlers' habit of sticking things in their ears and noses. Do not use styrofoam pieces because children "must" chew on these non-edible things, and the small pieces may be inhaled causing a very serious hazard. Sometimes there are cultural or philosophical objections to using food as play materials.

PLAY DOUGH

A toddler program without play dough is almost inconceivable. It is truly a "basic" play material for toddlers. The primary appeal of play dough, of course, is to the sense of touch. It feels good to squeeze, poke, roll and pound. Toddlers love poking holes in things with their fingers and play dough is perfect for this. Children also gradually absorb concepts of size, shape and length as they experience dough. For toddlers, play dough is *not* a creative "art" medium. They are not interested in making things. They are interested in the changes they can make in a substance. A very real benefit of play dough is that it is a very soothing, calming activity for children and usually holds their attention well. If you need a few minutes to get something done, like preparing for lunch, play dough will do the trick.

Play dough has advantages over several other modeling materials for toddlers. Modeling clay, or plasticene, is too hard for toddlers to manipulate when it is cold. Earth clay, or potters clay, can be very messy and is sometimes hard to get.

Purchased play dough has a nice texture, pretty colors and smells good, but play dough is very easy and inexpensive to make. Try these favorite recipes for homemade play dough for some different textures. Some people like to add cooking extracts or perfume to give the dough a fragrance. Be aware that this will make children more likely to taste it.

Play Dough Recipes

Uncooked Play Dough

Mix together 2 parts flour, 1 part water, 1 part salt. Add a little more flour if it is sticky. Store in a zip lock bag or covered plastic container. Add food coloring to the water for color.

Cooked Play Dough

4 cups flour
2 cups salt
4 tablespoons cream of tartar
4 cups water
2 tablespoons oil

Cook over medium heat, stirring constantly until stiff. Let cool and knead. Store in a zip lock bag or plastic container. Add food coloring to water for color. This dough is especially long-lasting.

Salt and Cornstarch Play Dough

1 cup cornstarch
1 cup salt
1 cup hot water
1/2 cup cold water

Mix hot water and salt in a pan and bring to a boil. Stir cold water into cornstarch. Add cornstarch mixture to boiling water, and cook over low heat, stirring constantly until it is stiff. Remove from heat and turn out onto a counter to cool. Knead until smooth and pliable.

Baking Soda and Cornstarch Play Dough

2 cups baking soda
1 cup cornstarch
1-1/3 cups warm water

Mix baking soda and cornstarch in a pan. Add water and stir until smooth. Bring it to a boil over medium heat. Remove from heat and pour onto a board to cool. Knead it when it is cool enough and store it in a plastic bag or container. Add food coloring to the water for color.

THINGS TO DO WITH PLAY DOUGH

Rainbow Dough

Make play dough in several different colors. Roll each into a long snake and stack them. Then slice them to give the child several colors to play with at once.

Warm Dough

What a special treat to play with homemade dough while it is still warm! Ahhhh! Play dough can also be heated briefly in a microwave oven. Especially nice on a cold day.

Poke Things in It

Toddlers love making things stand up in the dough like candles in a birthday cake. Possibilities: popsicle sticks, tongue depressors, large pegs, plastic drinking straws.

Animal Stand-Up

Let children press their play dough into a pancake and stand up small plastic animals in it.

Pounding Hammers

Toddlers sometimes enjoy pounding the dough with the small wooden mallets that typically come with pounding benches. To make it even more interesting, glue a texture, such as a piece of mesh onion bag to the pounding surface.

Make Impressions

All kinds of junk materials are fun for older toddlers to stick in the dough and pull out again to see what kind of mark they make. Jar lids, forks, a potato masher, a pine cone...all make interesting marks. Can the child later remember which object made which mark?

Cookie Cutters

These are rarely used by toddlers to cut out shapes. Usually they end up being used to pound dough. Sometimes toddlers notice the pattern of the impressions made in the dough. It is hard for the toddler to get the dough flat enough to use cookie cutters for their intended purpose. A rolling pin is difficult for toddlers.

Cut Play Dough

Show the child how to roll the play dough into long snakes. Then let the child snip off pieces with blunt scissors. Children who cannot yet cut paper successfully will be able to do this. Supervise closely because hair is amazingly easy to cut! Also let children cut play dough into small pieces using a plastic knife.

Play Dough Table Top

Make a large amount of play dough and roll it so that it covers the entire top of a small table. Have a basket of small plastic animals and things to make impressions with nearby. This can be an available "interest center" all morning long. Covering it tightly with plastic wrap when not in use, like when you're outside, helps to keep it from drying out.

TASTING

Toddlers taste everything whether you want them to or not. They *have* to. It's a very "oral" stage of development. Everything goes in the mouth.The first awareness to develop is to make sure that everything around is *safe* to taste, in other words, "babyproofing" your environment and using only non-toxic materials. Once you're beyond that, there are many ways to give toddlers and two-year-olds fun experiences tasting new things.

From time to time, not at mealtime but as a special activity, offer toddlers small amounts of interesting things to taste. Such things as a small slice of raw turnip, a chunk of fresh pineapple, peas just out of the pod, provide opportunities to build vocabulary and talk about how things feel and taste.

Of course, you can introduce new foods at mealtime too.

Cooking Projects

Cooking projects are lots of fun for children. Keep it very simple, and make sure they are all actively involved in the process. Watching an adult cook something will have little value for two-year-olds and will not hold interest. So let the child do the stirring, pouring, measuring, and chopping (use a plastic knife). Never mind if it's not exact. They will want to taste each individual ingredient as it goes in. Try to think of recipes that are immediately edible, not requiring cooking, baking or refrigerator time. Toddlers may not connect the final product with the process; therefore it's best to do very simple projects with one, two or three children at a time.

Some ideas for starters:

- Peanut butter and banana sandwiches
- Fresh orange juice and other fresh fruit juice
- Fruit salad, lettuce salad
- Instant pudding
- Pancakes
- Explore a fruit, cutting it into different shapes, and using it in different forms such as fresh, cut into chunks, juice, cooked sauce, jam, etc.

Mud Balls

Mix together and form into balls:
Peanut butter
Honey
Dry, powdered milk
Crushed graham crackers
Raisins
Frozen orange juice concentrate.

Roll in carob powder or dry instant chocolate drink mix. Other items may be added such as: cereal, unsweetened coconut, wheat germ, uncooked oatmeal.

Hints for Mealtime

- Take your time. Eating should be a leisure activity. It is a social, sensory and motor activity as well as simply getting nourishment.

- Offer snack outside and let them come and help themselves when they feel like it. (Have moistened towelettes for handwashing.)

- Create silhouettes of dishes, spoons and cups on paper and laminate them to the table top with clear self-adhesive paper. Toddlers will find it easier to set the table, if you have them help with that, and to replace their cups to a position where they are less likely to be knocked off the table.

- Table manners should be there, but relaxed. Remember that toddlers are the explorers and investigators of the childhood world. Their unspoken question for any object, including food, is "How can I make a toy out of this?" They are gaining physical knowledge about food, just as they would for any other object. What are manners, after all? They are behaviors that make it not disgusting to be at the same table with us. Many manners have cultural roots. However, rules that make no sense to toddlers are hard to remember and comply with. The best strategy is to sit down and eat at the same table with the children. You can restrict the more outrageous behaviors while modeling appropriate behavior. The purpose is to make it a relaxed, social, language-rich time.

- Food should never be used for *"behavior modification"* or withheld as punishment. Telling a child he won't have dessert if he doesn't clean up, or substituting a cracker while others have ice cream, for instance, puts undue importance on food. The child will learn to turn to food in order to feel good about himself and you could be laying the foundation for later eating disorders.

- You are helping children form *attitudes* about food. By offering them a variety of food in a relaxed, social setting, you help them develop habits of good nutrition and they are more likely to avoid eating problems in the future.

- Develop a routine for cleaning up afterwards. For instance, children could bring their dishes over to a tub, put their napkins in a waste basket, wipe their faces with a damp washcloth from a stack of clean moistened cloths, and then put their washcloths in another container.

Food for Family Involvement.

Food is a great way to bring people together. Potluck meals to which families bring food from their cultures are a fun way to celebrate who you are. Also invite families to share recipes or samples of food from their cultures for children to try during the day.

SMELLING

The world is full of interesting odors and aromas. Unlike tasting, feeling, making noises, and looking at things, toddlers do not consciously go up to something and smell it. But they *do* smell things.

Things to Smell

Collect some items with an interesting and distinct odor such as perfume, cedar shavings, spice bottles, and candles. Simply say, "I have something interesting for you to smell," and put it up to your own nose and smell it. Then put it under the child's nose. The child may quickly get the idea of what "to smell" means.

Smells are so closely associated with tasting that the toddler will immediately want to put the substance in his mouth, so do supervise, and say something like, "This is for smelling, not for tasting."

Go on a Smell Walk

Take a walk around the building or outside to discover different smells. You might "arrange" some smells ahead of time.

Food Smells

Whenever there is food around you have an opportunity to talk about smells. A popular game with older children is to blindfold them and let them guess what they are smelling or tasting. Most toddlers are afraid to have a blindfold tied over their eyes, so that kind of guessing game is not appropriate for this age. Older toddlers may cooperate if you say, "Close your eyes and try to guess what this is." Talk about the aromas of food yourself. "Mmmm...it smells like we're having spaghetti for lunch today."

Sniff Bottles

Wash out plastic squeeze bottles such as mustard and catsup dispensers or dishwashing liquid bottles. Put something with a strong scent inside or saturate a cotton ball with a liquid fragrance. Fasten the tops securely with glue or strong tape. Then show children how to squeeze the bottle to make a puff of air come out to sniff. Possibilities: almond extract, perfume, cloves, vinegar, lemon extract, garlic. Caution: toddlers will probably try to get the tops off to get at whatever is inside and taste it. Be sure that whatever you use is non-toxic, just in case they succeed. (You can expect a toddler to suck on anything that is remotely shaped like a baby bottle.)

LOOKING

A toddler's big expressive eyes take everything in. Toddlers have the full visual capabilities of an adult. If you suspect the child has a vision problem there are simple tests which a pediatrician or community health center can perform. Early detection is extremely important.

Here are some ways to have fun with the sense of sight:

Colored Windows

Tape colored cellophane on the window and the world will change color as the child wanders by.

Looking Tube

Look through a paper towel tube. You see the world in small sections and it looks different.

Colored Looking Tube

Put colored cellophane over the end of toilet paper tubes, securing it with a rubber band. Let the child look through.

Bottles of Colored Water

Put colored water (use food coloring) in clear plastic bottles and look through. Setting these in a sunny window will cast colored shadows.

Plastic Jug Looking Tube

Cut the bottom off a large plastic bleach bottle or milk jug and wash it out thoroughly. The child will enjoy looking through both ends.

Scarf Looking

Put a gauzy scarf over the child's head and see what the world looks like.

Mirror Images

Children enjoy studying their image in mirrors. Talk to the child in the mirror and help the child notice his friends.

Distorted Images

Distorted reflections in something like a shiny pot are fun for toddlers. One caregiver found a shiny hub cap and has it hanging low where toddlers can see themselves.

Flashlights

Put colored cellophane over the ends of flashlights and let children shine these in a darkened room. Flashlights without cellophane are fun too, of course!

FREQUENTLY ASKED QUESTIONS

How can I get the children to stop throwing the sand?

This usually happens when there are no shovels, pails, scoops or other sand toys to play with. Then, throwing the sand is the most exciting thing to do with it. Toddlers need a very firm statement from the adult when they throw sand. "Sand is not for throwing. Look, it hurt Jamal's eyes. He's crying. Sand is for digging...here is a shovel and pail. I will not let you throw sand." Then if the child persists, he must be removed from the sandbox.

What can we do about the mess? Children fill containers with sand and dump them in other parts of the yard, killing grass and making the sidewalks slippery. And inside the floor gets gritty.

You will need to give constant reminders, "The sand belongs in the box," etc. If you can find a small broom or cut down the handle of a larger one and provide a dust pan, children can sweep up their own spills.

I realize sand play is important, but how can I keep sand out of children's hair?

When sand gets in the hair of African American children it can be quite difficult to get out and parents sometimes request that their child not be allowed to play in sand. However, if children wear hats or bonnets outside, a good idea anyway, this problem can be greatly reduced. You could have a hat rack with a labeled hat **for each child** near the door that leads to the yard.

How can I keep the young toddlers from eating the sand?

The key to a successful sandbox is having interesting things to use there. It seems to be mostly "inexperienced" toddlers who eat sand – they are just exploring the media with *all* their senses. Sit down in the sandbox with the toddler and show him how to play in sand. Simply playing there as though you were a child yourself is all you need to do. The toddler will learn by imitation.

We keep losing the sand toys, and they get scattered all over the yard.

Keeping track of sand toys can be a problem. One solution is to have a "cleanup time" at the sandbox before going inside and put all of the toys back into a special container. A covered plastic garbage can attached to a tree, post, or fence works well. Or, use a box or laundry basket and bring it inside each day.

CHAPTER 12

Moving!

*I*t only takes Connor a few seconds to decide what he's going to do today... play on the slide. First he goes down sitting down. Then he tries climbing back up. How about head first? Backwards? He systematically uses his body in every way imaginable, negotiating the four-foot incline before he runs off to jump on the mattress in the corner of the room.

Physical activity is *the* dominant theme of children between one and three. Two-year-olds are considered the most active age of preschoolers. They *have to* move. They compulsively practice all of the new physical skills they are learning. The wise parent or caregiver will provide many legitimate, safe and fun ways for children to practice their new skills. Through all of these activities, children gain skill and coordination, which relates also to self-esteem. Allow children lots of active play.

CRAWLING AND HIDING IN SMALL PLACES

Why do toddlers like to be in and under things so much? Is it the comfortable memory of the prenatal period? We will never know! Undoubtedly as a child fits herself into a small space she is developing a sense of her own body and how much space she takes up. Concepts of space and location, such as *in, out, under, through, behind*...are slowly being absorbed as adults talk and describe where they are.

Nooks and Crannies

See how many small spaces you can create for a toddler to crawl in and out of in your environment. Some ideas:

• Cardboard grocery cartons. Simply put them in the room with toddlers and watch the fun.

• Empty plastic dish tubs on the floor entice a child to get inside.

• Put a pillow inside a big galvanized wash tub to create a cozy space.

• Lay an empty shelf unit on its back, giving children a fun trough to sit in.

- Throw a blanket over a table or some chairs lined up back to back to create a tunnel.

- Purchased fabric tunnels are very popular in toddler programs. You can also make a tunnel by taping together a number of large cardboard grocery boxes end to end.

- Make a playhouse out of a large cardboard appliance box.

- Put up a small tent.

- Hang a sheet over part of your climber.

A Counter Cave

Remove two cabinet doors under a counter and take out the shelves. Place a small foam mattress and some pillows inside. You could decorate the inside walls with pictures or a mirror.

WALKING

How Many Ways?

Challenge children to walk slowly, quickly, sway back and forth, march, stomp, tiptoe.

Going Around

Toddlers like to walk, run, jump, *around* a large object like a tree, a bush, a table, a chair or another child. One child might move a chair to a central spot and simply start walking around it. Often she is joined by one or two other children. Perhaps having a focal point object in the middle makes it easier to circle around and get back to where you started from. Perhaps it starts with children wanting to see what something looks like from the other side. Usually all you have to do is put on some music (even that is not really necessary) and say, "Let's walk around the table," and around they'll go. In the process they are learning what "around" means as well as seeing their environment from different perspectives.

Walk the Plank

Find a board about eight to twelve inches wide and four or five feet long. Place it flat on the floor. Challenge the child to walk all the way across it without stepping off. Try other ways of moving along the plank. Crawling should be easy. Older two-year-olds may be able to tiptoe across, step sideways, or even walk backwards.

CLIMBING

Toddlers and two-year-olds are compulsive climbers. They will scale anything available, including bookshelves, chairs, and tables. For the safety of life and limb as well as the preservation of furniture, it is highly desirable to provide children with something legitimate to climb. This is one instance where the purchase of one of the many available manufactured climbing structures is advisable because of the durable and safe construction offered by manufacturers. It's wise to have one of these inside, as well as an outside climbing structure. Put protective matting or cushions underneath inside, and make sure there is an approved cushioning surface under it outside, such as sand or pea gravel.

Learning to Use a Climber

Never put a child up on a climber. The child should climb up herself, or not be on it at all. Most accidents happen when a child has not gotten up there herself. If she becomes "stuck" or afraid to climb down, resist the temptation to simply "rescue" her and lift her off. Instead, try to show the child how to do it herself. You can put your hand on her hand or foot and guide it to a lower rung – step by step. "Oh – I see you are stuck, Briana. I'll help you figure this out. Put this foot down here. That's right! Now put this hand over here. This hand here now. Can you get down the rest of the way now? Good! You did it yourself." Instead of being a temporary solution you are thus helping the child develop skills and confidence.

Stairs

Young toddlers especially, and infants just learning to walk, are fascinated by stairs. It's important that you keep a gate across stairs to prevent falls. When you can, spend some time with a toddler on some stairs. Let the child enjoy the challenge of going up step after step with you right behind for safety. It is much harder for a toddler to go down stairs than to climb up. She will enjoy inventing her own way to go up and down with you close at hand for safety. A toddler will gradually learn to go up and down stairs in an upright posture, one step at a time. A "rocking boat" that inverts to a low set of steps, or some other small set of steps specifically designed for toddlers, is a useful manufactured piece of equipment to have.

RUNNING

Running and Falling

Slapstick humor has obvious appeal to two-year-olds, and running and purposely falling down seems to be a popular way they get other children to laugh. Provide a large pile of pillows or a mattress at one end of the room to give them a safe place to land.

The Chase Game

To play, say, "You chase me – I'm running away from you. Oh, no! You caught me! Now I'll chase you!" Expect squeals of delight. Much to a hurried parent's frustration, toddlers love to chase and be chased. If you make a legitimate game out of it perhaps you can say later when running away is not appropriate, "We're not playing chase now."

THROWING

Toddlers love to throw things. It's probably a fascination with the cause and effect phenomenon – pure physics. "I make my arm do this, open my hand at the proper moment, and the thing goes flying through the air. Wonderful!"

Stuff to Throw Box

The obvious thing is to have objects available that are okay to throw so you can redirect when children throw inappropriate things. Possibilities: bean bags (keep in good repair), yarn balls, soft "clutch balls," crocheted toys, foam rubber balls, stuffed animals, fabric covered foam blocks, small brown bags stuffed with wadded up newspaper and taped shut, pairs of socks in a ball.

Stocking Balls

Tie a knot at the bottom of a leg of a pair of pantyhose. Stuff a large handful of polyester stuffing material (available at sewing supply and variety stores) into the leg and down to the knot. Tie a knot above it and cut it off. One pair of panty hose can yield about 8 balls. These are great to throw, and they can be washed and dried in a washing machine and dryer. Or, stuff old socks for this purpose.

Targets

You might block off a corner of the room and challenge children to throw the things you give them into that corner. A laundry basket or large cardboard box make good targets, too.

PUSHING THINGS

One often sees toddlers pushing their own strollers in shopping malls. POWER! A very popular purchased toy is the little plastic shopping cart. Toddlers push them around endlessly, and they enjoy filling and emptying the basket, too.

Chair Train

Have children push a bunch of chairs together to make a train or bus. This activity is a sure hit.

Push a Friend on a Riding Toy

Toddlers like to give their friends a ride by pushing a riding toy. It's as much fun as being the rider. It's also a good way to learn about taking turns.

Pushing Boxes

If you provide empty grocery boxes, toddlers often choose to push them around the room. They could give dolls and stuffed animals a ride.

Toy Vehicles

Toy cars and trucks get much attention from toddlers. It's best to get durable toy vehicles because toddlers, even when they are way too big, will try to sit in or on them. Make sure wheels are securely attached. Trains are especially interesting to toddlers.

Children enjoy pushing toy vehicles along a ledge in a room, such as a windowsill or a shelf.

Push Toys

Commercially available push toys on the end of a stick remain popular with toddlers. These toys usually include a sound which gives children the added pleasure of a "cause and effect" response. Much of the appeal is also in imitating adults pushing a vacuum cleaner or mop.

PULLING

Wagon

A small sturdy wagon is a good toy for two-year-olds. They push it, pull it, load and unload it, and give toys and each other rides in it.

Dish Tub Train

Make a train by tying several dish tubs together. Let children give rides to dolls and stuffed animals.

SLIDING

A short slide is very exciting to toddlers. Children will seem to do a survey on how many ways one can go down a slide. Physics, gravity, and body awareness are experienced.

ROLLING

Rolling Things Down a Slide

You can put a box at the bottom of a slide and let children roll things down the slide and into the box. Toddlers like to watch toys go down a slide.

Rolling Around

It's hard for toddlers to lie on their side and roll over and over. Lateral torso muscles get new practice. Rolling down a grassy hill is a special pleasure if you have one available. But it's fun just rolling on the floor, too.

JUMPING

Once toddlers master standing and walking it seems that their next logical goal is to learn how to fly! Anyway, they sure jump a lot. In an attempt to jump, they don't always get completely off the ground, but they try. Here are some simple and fun jumping activities.

Hold Hands and Jump

Simple as it seems, this activity is a real winner! Just hold hands with a child and jump up and down – with or without music. You could chant, "Jump, jump, jump..." You could do this with several children at once in a circle.

Jingle Bell Anklets

Sew some jingle bells onto elastic that will fit a child's ankles comfortably. They love to jump up and down to music and make the jingle bells ring.

Jump Off a Low Platform

Have you noticed how toddlers like to jump off the bottom step of the stairs, or a curb, or the side of the sandbox? You could build a small wooden platform about six inches high for inside. Carpet it perhaps. They'll use it a lot!

Mattress

Place a box spring mattress covered with a sheet on the floor and allow children to jump up and down on it. Great fun!

SWINGING

Toddlers love to swing and they are learning more physics as they do so. Centrifugal force and gravity are felt with their whole body. Swings with soft "sling" seats and horizontal tire swings are safest for toddlers.

Swings need close adult supervision. Toddlers have absolutely no sense of the amount of space swings require and will walk right in front of them. It is a good idea to hang swings up over the top bar of the swing frame when they cannot be closely supervised.

One favorite activity is to swing back and forth, tummy down.

RIDING

Although tricycles are too advanced for toddlers and most two-year-olds, they greatly enjoy wheeled riding toys, propelling them with their feet on the ground. These toys can be used indoors and outdoors. When children ride these little scooters, cars, and trucks they are involved in valuable dramatic play while developing the coordination to later succeed with the pedals of a tricycle.

Road

You might try marking off a "road" on the floor, to cut down on reckless driving. This also provides the added challenge of steering the toy to stay within certain boundaries. If storage is a problem you might hang riding toys on a high pegboard when the room cannot tolerate heavy vehicular traffic.

Inner Tube

If you can find a large truck inner tube, several children at a time will have fun straddling it and bouncing up and down, pretending to ride a horse.

DIFFERENT MOVES

Obstacle Course

Make an obstacle course in your room by making a line of masking tape or yarn to follow under tables, around and behind shelves, pillows, etc. Demonstrate what to do and have children follow you. This is great to do on a bad weather day when you can't go outside and want to provide some exercise and a change of pace.

Follow the Leader Moves

Using the "Follow the Leader" technique, model for the children different ways to move. They will imitate you. Try: crawling, jumping, rolling, walking, walking on tiptoe, sliding sideways, dancing, waving your arms. You can add music. The beauty of this activity is it is immediately available, and children will always join you. It's irresistible.

FREQUENTLY ASKED QUESTIONS

When would you call a child hyperactive at this age?

Because this is such an extremely active age, many parents have feared that their child is "hyperactive" or ADHD. Most pediatricians will not make this diagnosis until the child is older. At any rate, slapping on a label will not change the situation. Instead, respond to the child's behavior. Remembering that good "curriculum" starts where the child is, allow this child lots and lots of very active play. If possible, increase the outside play time. Provide for plenty of allowable inside active play. Do the "flop and do" technique, rather than requiring that all children sit still and pay attention at the same time, and limit the amount of time you require this child to be still and inactive. Think of ways to offer learning activities "on the move."

CHAPTER 13

Peek-A-Boo

Young toddlers love activities that involve covering something up and uncovering it again or hiding something and quickly rediscovering it. At the age of about nine months infants acquire "object permanence." They make the amazing discovery that something still exists even when they can no longer see it. Until then, if you hide an attractive toy under a blanket or behind a box, the infant will no longer look for it. "Out of sight, out of mind." But at some magical stage of mental development the child will push the box aside or pull the blanket to retrieve the toy, indicating that there was still a mental image of the toy when it was out of sight. Toddlers still love to "test" this. A spontaneous game of peek-a-boo will often turn a cranky and fussing toddler into a giggling child.

Classic Peek-A-Boo

Put your hands in front of your face. Open them out like the doors on a cuckoo clock and say "Peek-a-boo" and close them again. Do this repeatedly and you will get the smiles and attention of young toddlers. Best of all, you can probably get the toddler to do it too. "Now you do it."

Use a Scarf

A thin scarf held in front of the child's face and quickly pulled away will be a favorite. It is not threatening, because they can still see what's out there.

Curtain on a Climber

Attach a sheer curtain to a climber or loft, so that a child can go behind it and "hide" himself. You can play along. "Where's Jimmie? Peek-a-boo! I found you!"

Clothing

Toddlers have often been seen to do this with clothing, their coats, security blankets and bedding. Many toddlers do not like clothing that must be pulled over their heads – even undershirts. Saying "peek-a-boo" when the head pops out may defuse the anger.

Barriers

Popping up and down from behind a chair or shelf is also fun. Children quickly learn to do this themselves. This may be one of the first forms of social interactions between children of the same age. Puppets, teddy bears, and dolls are also very good at playing peek-a-boo.

Mirror with a Curtain

Rig up a curtain over a mirror. (It's always good to have a low mirror where toddlers can see themselves.) The child will enjoy pulling the curtain aside and saying "Peek-a-boo" to his own image.

Doll Blankets

One of the things toddlers most often do with dolls, given the opportunity, is to cover and uncover the doll with a small blanket. This is a form of a peek-a-boo game for toddlers.

Books

When you think about it, turning the pages of a book is a form of a peek-a-boo activity. Watch a toddler with a book for a few minutes – it's the "mechanics" of the book that first intrigue the child. Turn the page – the picture goes away – then turn it back and it appears again! You will notice that toddlers often turn the same page back and forth, back and forth. This is one reason it makes sense to have books around that toddlers are allowed to handle themselves.

Flap Book

Tape together two pieces of cardboard so they will close like a book. Glue a picture on the inside. A sequence of these could also be attached to a vertical surface at child level. The child can lift up the flaps as he walks by. You could use sheer or opaque fabric for the top flap for variety.

Peek-A-Boo Books

These are the books that have little doors to open on the pages to reveal something underneath. You could also make books like these from cloth or cardboard. Toddlers love these kinds of books, but they should probably be used exclusively on an adult's lap because toddlers also tend to tear off the flaps. Other books have little pockets in them to put things in.

Peek-A-Boo Guessing Book

Use small spiral bound index cards for this. Glue a full page picture of a familiar object or scene to every other page, starting with the second page. Cover all the pages on both sides with clear self-adhesive paper. Cut the pages with no pictures on them into several horizontal strips, going from the edge of the page to the spiral binding.

When you look at this book with the child, turn one strip at a time, gradually revealing more and more of the picture underneath. Let the child guess what the picture is.

Suitcases

A small suitcase or briefcase is an ideal thing to put with other dramatic play materials for toddlers. They will love packing and unpacking it and lugging it around. Part of the appeal of playing with a suitcase is to discover that the things inside are still there when the suitcase is opened up again. They will also be fascinated with the latches.

Peek-A-Boo Puzzles

These are wooden inlay puzzles that have individual pieces with knobs on them to make them easier for small hands to remove. Under each puzzle piece is another picture. This adds motivation and appeal to the puzzle. A child is usually approaching two before he can work such a puzzle without help.

The Old Shell Game

Take three containers – cans or cups would work nicely – and put a small toy under one. Move them slowly to change their positions while the child watches. Can he pick the one that has the toy under it?

Bury Things in the Sandbox

Sit down next to the toddler in the sandbox and show him how to dig a small hole, put a small object in it, and cover it up with sand again. Then ask, "Where's the car?" When the child removes the sand to discover the object, express delight: "There's the car!"

Unwrapping and Peeling Things

Taking the paper off presents, opening boxes, finding "surprises" in shopping bags, even peeling oranges, eggs, or bananas have an element of "peek-a-boo."

Latch and Lock Board

These are very popular toys because toddlers love to manipulate small things with their fingers. They also enjoy the hinge effect of the little doors. If you add little pictures or a mirror behind the doors you will add the peek-a-boo appeal. Keep these in good repair, or better yet, make your own.

A Simple Doorboard

Two large pieces of posterboard, some glue and some magazine pictures are all you need for this. Cut a number of little doors in one piece of posterboard. Place this over the second piece of posterboard and trace around the holes where the doors are. Remove the top board and glue magazine pictures in the spaces traced from the door holes. Then glue the top piece of posterboard with the doors onto the bottom piece. Children will love to open the little doors to see what's underneath. You could attach a little loop of yarn to make the door easier to open.

Countdown Calendars

Using the same construction as for the "Doorboard" described above, you could actually make one of these to anticipate any coming event such as a birthday, a trip to the zoo or when daddy comes home from a business trip. There is a numbered door for each waiting day. The child opens one door each day. There is a topic related picture under each door. In addition to the fun of revealing pictures under the doors, it may begin to give the child a feeling for the passage of time and what a day and a week is...although full understanding of time will not come for several years. Older children will get practice using numbers in the correct sequence.

Match Boxes

Small match boxes with little "drawers" that slide out fascinate toddlers both because of the mechanics and because of what's inside of them. Remove the matches. You could glue different textures of materials inside the drawers, such as cotton, sandpaper, chamois, sponge, etc. You could also glue attractive pictures into the match box drawers. Reinforcing the outside of the match box with pretty self-adhesive paper will also increase its durability. It's fun because the toddler can make the thing inside appear and disappear by pushing the drawer in and out.

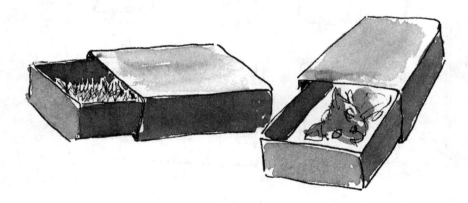

Toddler Hide and Seek

This is a thrilling game greatly enjoyed by toddlers. When children aren't looking, simply hide yourself and call out, "I'm hiding...come and find me!" Leave part of you sticking out and visible. Children will learn to follow the direction of your voice. Do they associate one visible shoulder and arm with the whole body attached to it? What a thrill when they find you...a good excuse for a hug! Eventually you can invite a child to hide himself. Does he know what it means? Sometimes the child will think he is hiding but is almost completely visible to other children. To hide successfully a child must develop a sense of the space of his own body and must also start to think about how something would look from someone else's point of view...very difficult for toddlers.

Who's Under the Sheet?

Have children close their eyes or turn their backs. Cover up one child with a small sheet or blanket. Then let the others feel the sheet and try to guess who is under it. You can give clues by exposing a shoe, part of the hair, etc. This game is more difficult than it may seem. Children have to maintain a mental image of the other child. It works only when all the children know each other well, and when children are at least two-and-one-half years old. Even if it's not totally successful, it's still fun being under the sheet and being the center of attention!

Hide a Toy

When children come in from outside, or wake up from naps (or anytime) you might say, "I have hidden Teddy Bear. Can you find him?" Leave part visible. They have to remember what the toy looks like and must use a certain amount of reasoning in the process.

Pockets

Children love exploring your pockets for hidden treasures. You could create a pocket apron with lots of different sizes and shapes of pockets with small things inside. Put different things in the pockets each day.

Fingerpaint on a Mirror

Use shaving cream or fingerpaint with liquid detergent added for a fun "peek-a-boo" art activity.

FREQUENTLY ASKED QUESTIONS

How does playing "peek-a-boo" relate to academic learning?

The main benefit is learning to keep a mental image of the thing that is not visible. The child has to be skillful at developing pictures in his mind and remembering attributes to later do mathematics and learn to read.

While hide and seek is usually fun, it can be very irritating when the child does this at the end of the day when a hurried parent is trying to get the child home.

True! The child is using this game to "engage" the parent after being separated for a long time. This type of "chase" game involves some safe risk, allowing the parent to appear and disappear...but now the child, not the parent, is in control. Here we are again, back to the prevalent issue of power! Maybe the parent could be the one who initiates the game and "hides" and then when the child finds her, she can catch him!

CHAPTER 14

Mimicking and **P**retending!

*I*n the normal, routine func-tioning of the "free play" time in the toddler room *Tomeo gets down on all fours and says, "Meow, meow." The teacher says, "Oh, look, Tomeo is pretending to be a kitty. I bet I can be a kitty too." Soon there are numerous kitties crawling around the floor.*

Lunch is over and the teacher is wiping the table with a damp cloth. Next to her are several children who are also wiping the table with damp cloths. The teacher bends over to pick up a piece of food that has fallen on the floor. The children also look for fallen food and pick up crumbs.

A young child talks to "Daddy" on a toy telephone. Another child "reads" a storybook to her teddy bear.

"Monkey see, monkey do." Mimicking behavior seems to be a basic learning style for primates – and toddlers are the champions for humans. Toddlers are learning that they are separate human beings and are constantly making the dis-covery, "I can do that too!" "My body will work that way too." "I can make a sound just like that!" Their self-esteem grows as they discover more and more things they can do

"Just like Mommy" (or Daddy, or Teacher or friends.) So, if you want to get a toddler to do something, just start doing it yourself. It's a very effective teaching strategy.

MIMICKING

Follow the Leader Games

Many simple variations of "Follow the Leader" will find success with toddlers. You don't have to announce the game, or appoint a leader or have everybody participate. Just start imitating someone else or start doing something yourself.

- Call attention to a child's unusual actions and start doing it yourself.

- Clap your hands and tap the other parts of your body and children will mimic you. You can name the body parts as you do this.

- Start dancing when you hear music and you'll have a bunch of dancers.

- This is even a way to have children help clean up. Make it look like fun and perhaps accompany yourself with a song: "I'm putting the pegs in the box, box, box, and Jasmine is helping me too."

Funny Noises

Make funny noises of any type and watch children mimic you. You mimic their noises, too. Don't limit yourself to voice noises. Tongue clicking, clapping, tapping hollow cheeks, stomping are other sounds to make and mimic.

Can You Do What I Do?

Make your own melody to this chant:

Can you do what I do, I do, I do...
Can you do what I do, just like me...?

Do different actions and watch children imitate you.

Later, when children are very familiar with this game, a child can be the leader. "Can you do what Jenny does, Jenny does, Jenny does..." etc. However, if you go from one child to another to have them take turns being the leader, you can expect them all to do the same action the first child did. You might decide this is okay. It's wonderful for the ego to be the leader and have everyone copy you, no matter what you do.

DRAMATIC PLAY

Mimicking adult behavior is basic to dramatic play or "pretend play." A toy telephone is usually one of the first toys we see toddlers use for this purpose. A child as young as eight months will put a toy phone receiver to her ear and happily babble into it. "Pretending," using one object to symbolize something else, represents the very beginning of abstract thinking in young children. Do toddlers realize that they will be grown-ups one day? They seem to, as they closely observe adults and imitate them in their play.

Dramatic play can be greatly enhanced in value if an adult or school age child plays with the toddler, giving words and structure to the play. It especially delights toddlers if you occasionally play the "baby."

THE VALUE OF DRAMATIC PLAY

- **Emotional.** We're back to the theme of "power" again. Children usually take on roles of power when they pretend. They become the truck driver who controls the big, noisy, scary truck, the doctor who gives the shots, the parent who tucks the unwilling child in bed. Since young children have little power in their real life, this can be important.

- **Empathy.** When children play a role and pretend to be someone else, they gain valuable practice in feeling what it would be like to be someone else.

- **Self-image.** They can try out what it would be like to be a powerful person or a scary monster, gaining some feelings of control over powerful feelings inside themselves.

- **Vocabulary.** Expressive language is enhanced, especially when children are interacting with other children in their play. They have to make their ideas known to the others.

- **Using symbols.** Toy play props are symbols of the real thing. And as children invent their own props, like using a plate for a steering wheel, they are making their symbols more abstract. This relates to later using other abstract symbols like letters and numbers to represent something else.

- **Pre-reading.** When children act out their own scenes in play, such as going to the doctor, they gain skill in following the plot of a story.

- **Social.** When they pretend play with other children, they have to pay attention to the other child and what she or he is doing, and fit their own actions to what is going on, sometimes negotiating their own wishes.

DRAMATIC PLAY SKILL PROGRESSION

Mimicking. The play of toddlers is mostly simple mimicking – imitation of what they have seen others do, copying the actions and postures of adults.

Taking on a role. The next step is to pretend to be someone else. The child will start to talk like someone she is pretending to be. You will notice a change in tone of voice and facial expressions.

Solitary play. Much pretend play of toddlers is solitary – in their own little world.

Parallel play. Given the opportunity to play with other children, they will start to imitate what another child is doing, not necessarily interacting with that child. You will see sound effects and actions imitated. Both children are doing the same thing.

Interacting. Very gradually, and usually after the toddler period, when the child has good language skills, she will start to have some give and take with another child, acting from within a role, such as a "mother" asking "the doctor" questions about the sick doll.

Use of props. Young toddlers simply respond to whatever "prop" is available, for instance, picking up a telephone and pretending to talk, or pushing a toy lawn mower to pretend to cut grass, or pretending to eat realistic looking plastic food. Later the child learns to use gestures to pretend, or can use something more abstract, like a block for a telephone.

Planning. Toddlers do not plan. They just respond to what is there. An older child will have an idea of a situation she wants to recreate, such as a fire, and will gather props and people needed.

HOW TO ENHANCE DRAMATIC PLAY

Provide interesting props. Since toddlers respond to what is there, be conscious of giving them a variety of interesting objects to play with over time that will encourage different types of roles.

Play with them. A child's ability to pretend increases with experience. A four-year-old who has had little interaction with other children or playful adults may play like a toddler at first. But a two-year-old who has had lots of experience playing will have advanced play skills. You won't be able to play with children all the time, and sometimes you'll prefer to stand back and observe, but join in occasionally, and see if you can extend the level of the play.

Talk for dolls. Use a "doll voice" and talk about how the doll feels in that situation. "Oh...I don't like it down here on the floor. I hope someone picks me up soon..." The children will pick up this skill quickly and learn about empathy in the process.

Take assignments. Let the child decide what role you will play. It will likely be the less powerful role, like the baby who is sick and must get the shot.

Ask extending questions. "What are we pretending here?" "Will we need to get gas for our car?" "What will we need to bring along for our picnic? What could we use?"

Involve others. Invent corresponding roles for other children to get them used to interacting with each other in their play. "We need a bus driver over here." "Maria and I are going on a picnic. Does anyone want to come along?"

Help them invent props. "We don't really have a bus. What could we use to pretend?"

Observe. When play is going fine without your help, just observe what is going on and take a note or two to record children's progress in play skills and the themes they seem to be playing out.

SOME GOOD PROPS FOR TODDLER PRETEND PLAY

Dramatic play toys and props need to be simple and quite realistic for toddlers. A real pot, a wooden spoon, and something to "stir" like large wooden beads will draw the attention of a toddler. Playhouse furniture will get much use.

Dishes

Instead of buying miniature play dishes which sometimes break easily, give toddlers the real thing – some old plastic tableware and pots and pans. Perhaps you can pick some up at a garage sale.

Cans and Boxes

Save empty cans and boxes you use in your own cooking. Clean them and make sure there are no sharp edges. The boxes especially will get damaged as children play with them. Just throw them away and replace them with new ones. The ever-changing variety will keep interest high.

Stove and Sink

Most toddler programs have a child-sized set of kitchen appliances. There are many manufacturers of this type of furniture. It's worth it to buy the sturdier, more expensive type for group care. I have also seen fine homemade appliances. You don't have to be elaborate if you don't want to spend a lot of money. You can paint "burners" on a simple board, add a few knobs and have an adequate stove. A dish tub with a dish drainer next to it will be recognizable as a sink.

Dolls

Sturdy, well-made dolls are best – with arms and legs that will not come off easily because toddlers are not gentle with dolls. Dolls with rubber bodies are best so toddlers can bathe them. Try to get a male doll as well as a female doll. Boys like playing with dolls, too.

Cloth dolls and stuffed animals have always been loved by toddlers. Stuffed animals can easily be given a male name and balance the preponderance of female dolls. And you can make male cloth dolls.

Doll Bed

Putting the baby to bed is something a toddler has certainly watched an adult do and is something they like to imitate in play. Make sure the doll bed is large enough and sturdy enough for a child to get into, for they surely will try, even if the bed is way too small. Lacking a doll bed, you could use a large cardboard box. The bedding is more interesting. A small pillow and blanket or two will get much action from toddlers. Small dish towels make good doll blankets with which to cover the baby and tuck it in.

Dress-up Clothes

Dress-up clothes must be easy for toddlers to get on and off. Cut them down so they don't drag on the floor. Front buttons can be replaced with Velcro. Hats are a big hit with toddlers! Gather a big collection of all kinds of hats. You can buy a hat collection from suppliers, but you can usually scrounge some for free. Hats are easy to get on and off and what fun to see yourself transformed by a wonderful headdress! Shoes are fascinating to toddlers and those they can slip their feet into, shoes and all, are best. Big, furry animal slippers are a hit. Keep your eye open for other fun items such as ski goggles with the plastic removed, fancy scarves, ballerina tutus and perhaps a lovely fright wig.

A Mirror

A large unbreakable mirror is a good thing to have. It will find many uses as children develop their self-image, and the child can check out the effect of the dress-up clothes.

Purses, Etc.

Remembering how toddlers like to fill and empty containers and carry things around, purses are perfect for this compulsion. Also collect lunch boxes, a briefcase, shopping bags and other such containers with handles. It's a good idea to have a box of "purse junk" available to put in purses. Otherwise, toddlers will find other things such as crayons and puzzle pieces. Old keys, wallets, check books, junk mail, combs, empty lipstick containers, appeal to children because they are used by adults.

Shopping Bag Center

Get three or four shopping bags with handles and hang them low, where children can reach them. Put small objects in the bags and change them frequently. The objects might include junk mail, clothespins, small toys such as plastic animals, clean rocks, and shells. No object should be small enough for a child to choke on.

Strollers and Carts to Push

Pushing things is a toddler compulsion. A sturdy doll stroller is a good purchase. Another very popular toy in toddler programs is the small grocery cart children can push around.

Miscellaneous Enrichments

Props such as dish towels, dish drainers, pot holders, cloth napkins, plastic flowers in an unbreakable vase, a real telephone, magazines, etc., add realism to toddlers' dramatic play. Putting out different things from time to time will keep novelty and interest high.

A Window Scene

If you want to add a touch of "hominess" to the decor of your house corner, a window scene is fun. Find a large poster of an outdoor scene, or draw one yourself. Cover with clear self-adhesive paper and attach to the wall about three feet up from the floor. You could attach a curtain rod to the wall and hang real kitchen curtains. Or, cut curtain shapes out of checkered contact paper and stick this on over the scene.

FREQUENTLY ASKED QUESTIONS

When children pretend play, they just seem to be interested in the objects. How do I know if they're really taking on a role?

Toddlers have "object hunger." Much of their play is simply exploring the properties of objects. They probably have to do this first before they can use the objects in more abstract ways for pretend play, so do allow them plenty of time to do this. By playing along with them some of the time and prompting them, you can lead them into taking roles. Call the child by a role name. "Oh, *Mommy*, will you feed me some dinner? I'm so hungry."

Left to their own devices, the children playing with each other all just do the same thing.

"Parallel play" and solitary play are the most common types of social organization in the play of toddlers. In parallel play, you might have three mommies who are bathing three babies. Try to accommodate this by having several of the items needed for the play. They are actually picking up ideas from each other in this process and are having a successful play experience. When you play along with them, you can teach them how to take on different roles and interact in more complex ways, which they will do on their own as they gain experience.

CHAPTER 15

Making Friends

*J*oshua, sixteen months, and Timmy, fourteen months, are "buddies." They have been together with the same child care provider since early infancy. Their faces brighten up when they see each other. They seek to play near each other. One morning Joshua is late in arriving. Timmy is playing on the other side of the room, busily emptying a shelf. When Timmy notices Joshua and his dad come in, he issues a squeak of delight, and although he walks, he drops to all fours and quickly crawls across the room toward Joshua. Joshua, who sees him coming, picks up a small toy and hands it to Timmy.

No words are spoken, yet contact is established. Toddlers are "instrumental." They have "object hunger." They relate through objects. The gesture of handing over a toy is a way of saying, "Hey – I'm glad to see you. Let's play."

The last chapter in the book, this one might be considered the most important. It all leads to this – learning to get along with others and feel like a valued member of the group. People have always seen social development as the major benefit of group play situations for toddlers. It has become apparent through the tragic outbreak of violence in school settings in recent years that being able to have friends and feel a strong sense of self-worth in social settings are critically important life skills. Like everything else, these skills have their seeds of beginning in the toddler years.

Experience is needed to develop social skills. A child who has never had the opportunity to play with other children, at age five will be awkward in social settings.

Humans are social beings. As a species, we cannot get along independently. We need other people. There are mechanisms built into human development, such as bonding in infancy and language, that connect us to each other so that we survive. There is pleasure associated with social interactions, an attraction that is instinctive. We seek out others. But as anyone who has spent time around toddlers knows, the road is not always smooth. Toddlers want to have friends, but they can be very "bumbling" in their attempts at social interactions. They need a supportive adult to pave the way.

Where They're Coming From –
Beginnings in the Infant Year

We see social development – the interest in other human beings – from the very earliest stages of infant development. The newborn baby has a strong interest in faces. He stares strongly into his mother's face while nursing. A survival of the species mechanism, this gaze "captures" the caring adult who is then bound into service of the infant. The infant and a small circle of caring adults, with the mother at the center, form an attachment or "bond," a strong emotional tie. The adult cares for and protects the baby. The baby seeks comfort and security from the adult.

The social smile that develops at about three months of age strengthens the bonds with familiar adults. And while they will smile at any face, even that of a teddy bear, they smile stronger and longer for the mothers and others with whom they have a close bond. They radiate undiluted pleasure at the sight of other people.

Young infants also have a strong interest in the faces of other children. They are attracted to children's voices, and it is often a sibling who is most skilled at getting the baby to laugh. The infant enjoys being near other children and will watch them with interest.

At the beginning of toddlerhood, children learn to make gestures of friendship toward each other, as illustrated in the scenario above.

What Friendship Looks Like in the Toddler Years

Toddlers need to know each other – to be "used to" each other – in order for friendship behaviors to develop. Cousins, neighborhood playmates, child care pals can learn to interact with each other in playful ways. Depending on their basic temperament, it may take toddlers anywhere from weeks to months to warm up to each other.

First You See Simple Interest

A toddler new to a group will likely sit on the sidelines and watch the others play with interest, sizing up the situation. The child has to feel safe to venture out. So he spends time observing, to get some sense of predictability to the situation. How is she likely to react? What can I do to get her attention?

Help by simply allowing this to happen and don't force the child to participate if he seems content, but be there to help if the child seems eager to play with the others.

Solitary Play, but Close By

The child moves in, close to other children, playing by himself with a toy, not interacting with other children, just part of the social circle.

Help by staying close to make sure children don't push and crowd and the experience of playing near others is a pleasant one.

The Social Gesture

That first social entree – the signal, "I want to play" – can vary. Often it is exactly the wrong thing: the child barges in and interrupts or messes up whatever the other child was working on, or attempts to take something away. Here is where an adult can be extremely useful, moderating these early social attempts.

Help by recognizing the awkward gesture as an attempt for

social interaction, and give the child some better ideas, such as doing something similar to what the other children are doing close by, or imitating the actions and sounds of the other children. Tell the other children, "Look, Jimmy wants to play with you."

Handing an Object

The scenario at the beginning of the chapter shows a typical interaction. Toddlers often think of this themselves.

You can also initiate this with a toddler, and even make a game of handing a toy back and forth. An extension would be to hand objects back and forth with several children at once.

Imitative Parallel Play

The child picks up on what the other child is doing and imitates actions. There may be eye contact. One child hits the sand with a shovel, the other child imitates. One child makes vehicle noises while riding on a riding toy. The other child finds a riding toy, follows along, and makes the same kinds of noises.

Help by noticing out loud. "Wyatt is making the same noises that Eli is making." You could also join in such a game. "You two are falling backwards off of this log. That looks like fun. I think I'll do it too. You are fun to play with. You have good ideas." See how many of these spontaneous "toddler invented games" you can notice during a day.

Swarming

Toddlers are such "groupies" that when somebody starts doing something that looks interesting they all want to do it and you suddenly have a crowd of little bodies. They don't plan ahead much, but simply act on impulse. "That looks like fun. I want to do it too."

Since this can lead to pushing and frustration, you need to manage swarming. Divide and conquer. Get something else interesting going to draw off some of them. Also use this tendency to your advantage when you want them all to do something, like dance or march inside from the playground. Get several children started, make it look like fun, and others will follow.

Ringleaders

Certain children, just by their personal "charisma," are copied by others. These are usually the exuberant and slightly mischievous ones. They have good ideas, and usually fairly well developed social skills, so they are fun to be around.

Channel these children in positive directions, building on their social skills so that they are good for the others to emulate. Help them develop their good ideas. Redirect the ones that might cause trouble, like throwing stones over the fence, into something like tossing balls into a basket.

Interactive Play

True interactive play in which children exchange ideas and build off of each other develops slowly with two-year-olds. It is greatly helped when an adult plays along as a co-player, making suggestions, modeling how it is done, and modeling how to pick up on others' ideas. "Sandi picked up the picnic basket. Does that mean we're going on a picnic, Sandi? Joey, what shall we bring on our picnic? Who will drive the car? Is everybody ready? Let's get in the car so Joey can drive us to the beach."

The Influence of Language

Children's expressive language abilities have a great influence on their social skills. The more they can state their point of view, the less aggression there will be, and more cooperation and social give and take with others.

Your role as a coach is nowhere more important than here. Constantly work on giving children the phrases they need to get their point across. Model for them to parrot phrases like, "I have this now. You can have it in a minute." "I don't like that." "May I have a turn when you're through?" The day will come when they can use these phrases without your help, which will feel very gratifying for you.

LEARNING TO SHARE AND TAKE TURNS

"Mine!" The cry of toddlerhood! Sharing is hardly even an "emerging skill" for toddlers. Struggles over toys or space is often what leads to outbreaks of aggression. We've all seen toddlers who rigorously defend every toy at home, howling in protest if another child touches one. And we've all seen toddlers who insist on grabbing another child's toy even though there's a whole room full of perfectly good toys no one is using. There is a long road in front of you. It takes a long time and many gently guided experiences to learn to share. Very gradually it will sink in.

One problem with sharing at this age is that children have not yet learned to take another child's point of view. Their experience with other people is so limited that they think everyone sees things exactly the way they do. Since Jeffrey wants the truck, he thinks everyone else wants him to have the truck too, and he is genuinely surprised when there is a protest at the other end of the truck.

Paul and the Ball

Here is a true scenario very typical of toddlers:

Paul is a new child in the toddler group. It's his third day there and he's doing okay, although not talking much. He spots a ball on a shelf in the bathroom, points to it and shouts, "Ball!" The teacher takes it down and puts it in the room for the children to play with. Another older, larger child immediately grabs the ball, runs to the rocking boat, puts it in and sits on it, making sure Paul cannot touch it. (Pecking order being established.)

The teacher suggests the children sit in a circle with her and have fun rolling the ball to each other. The enticement of the teacher as a playmate gets cooperation. About six children choose to join her, including the ball possessor. She holds out her hands and says, "Roll me the ball!" Paul's face shows great anticipation. The ball is rolled back and forth between children. The second time the teacher gets the ball she rolls it to Paul. He grabs it eagerly and holds it. Everyone looks at him. The teacher holds her hands out. "Roll the ball to me, Paul!" No response. The other children hold their hands out. "Ball!" Paul hangs on. "We'll roll it right back to you!"

He *cannot* let go of the ball. Clearly, this is an issue of trust. The teacher decides not to take the ball away from him. "It looks like Paul needs to hold that ball now. Let's toss this foam block to each other instead." That sounds good to the other kids and they throw the soft block back and forth, grabbing it if it lands near them. After a few minutes, lo and behold, Paul rolls the ball to the teacher! She rolls the ball back to him immediately, and claps when he gets it, holds her hands out expectantly and he rolls it back. She sends it right back to him and claps. He rolls it back. She then rolls it to someone else, and the game continues a few minutes more with everyone clapping when someone catches the ball. Paul had to give up the ball on his own terms. Slowly the foundations of trust were being developed.

In order to share something, a child first has to possess it... really feel the ownership of it. Overpowering him and taking the thing away will produce a scream of outrage, and may prolong the child's learning of the ability to share willingly. Since the attention of toddlers is so easily distracted it's often best to offer the other child a different toy assuring that the first child will share the toy "when he's ready." It helps if you can play with the child who is waiting because that adds attractiveness to the second toy. Be sure to praise a child when he is finally able to share the coveted item.

Sharing and Taking Turns are Different Things

"Sharing" means using the same materials at the same time. For instance, if two children were to share a wagon, they would both be riding in it at the same time, or one would be pulling while the other ride. Both are using the wagon simultaneously.

"Taking turns" means one person waits while the other person uses the desired thing. Then they switch roles. One child pulls a load of dolls around the playground while the other waits. Then the child who is pulling turns over the wagon to the waiting child and waits while the child who was formerly waiting pulls the wagon.

Both are difficult for toddlers, however sharing can be accomplished more easily than taking turns, unless there is skillful adult help.

Teach What "Share" Means

Telling children, "You have to share," has little effect if they don't know what it means. Often, what children learn is that they lose the thing they are playing with because the adult confuses sharing and taking turns. Two children fight over the red truck. The adult intervenes and takes the truck away from the child who is clinging to it and gives it to the grabbing child, saying, "You have to share."

Instead, give children positive, successful, fun ways to share things. Bring in a snack that children like and say, "I'm going to share these crackers with you." Sit down next to a child playing with play dough and ask, "Would you share your play dough with me so I can play too?" When the child complies, thank him and say how much fun you are having. Make it more fun for him in the process.

Individual Projects, Shared Materials

Try seating two children at a table, giving each his own sheet of paper and putting a common bowl of crayons between them. You can also do this with the large rubber pegboards and put a bowl of pegs between the children. This could be done with other manipulative toys such as fit-together toys or table blocks. You could give each child a tray to work on and put a dish tub of toys between them. This technique usually works very well because there are lots of crayons or toys in the container of things to be shared instead of just one coveted item. The children enjoy the social contact with each other. The caregiver can make children conscious of sharing in a positive light. "You two can share these crayons, so you can *both* color."

Group Art Activities

Tape a large sheet of paper to the wall or a table top. Let several children scribble or paint on this surface at the same time. This is an experience where children are still "doing their own thing," but are using the same space. They are becoming aware of each other and you can talk about how they are sharing the paper and the crayons to make something together.

Teach About Taking Turns

Children don't come into the world knowing about delayed gratification and its many benefits. It doesn't make any sense to them. Why should they turn over the riding toy and cool their heels? Creating warm feelings of gratitude in their play partner is not much of a motivation for a two-year-old. So, you, the coach, have to show them the benefits and teach them the processes involved. This happens best in the heat of the situation. Notice a struggle and assist them in the process. Supply them words to parrot, and help make the words work.

- **Ask for a turn.** "Jordan, if you want to ride the truck you can't just pull Bradley off. That makes him mad. It works better if you ask for a turn. Ask Bradley, 'Can I have a turn?'"

- **Be understood.** "Bradley, did you hear Jordan? He wants to know if he can have a turn when you're through. Will you tell him when it's his turn?"

- **Answer the request.** "Jordan, Bradley says you can ride in a few minutes when he's done."

- **Do something interesting in the meantime.** "I'll help you wait. I'll push you on the swing while you wait for your turn."

- **Switch places.** "Bradley, would you like me to push you on the swing now? Jordan, Bradley is through with the truck."

- **Appreciate.** "Thank you, Bradley. You made Jordan feel good when you let him have a turn."

- **Show the benefit.** "You two did a great job taking turns. Both of you had fun with the truck, and both of you had fun on the swing."

Play a "Taking Turns" Game

This is a game that children can actually enjoy tremendously. You suggest the game before children are fighting over a toy or activity. It is a form of play-acting. Your pet puppet will love to direct this and make it even more fun with exaggerated expressions. Find something very simple for children to do...like give dolls a ride in a wagon around the sandbox on the playground – one time. The puppet could come out and announce the game. "Who wants to play 'Taking Turns' with me? Good! There are three of us! Here's what we'll do. First Jamie will pull the wagon around the sandbox, and then I'll say who's next. There he goes! He's at the other end of the sandbox. Now he's coming back. He's here! Now it's Tanisha's turn. Jamie's making the handover – there goes Tanisha!" The puppet can carry on an ongoing commentary, leading the others in clapping or singing, and cheer as the wagon is turned over each time. Make sure each child gets numerous turns. The puppet can also talk about how much fun it is to take turns.

Use a Timer

Two-year-olds can learn to trust the fairness of a kitchen timer if it used consistently and they are familiar with this way of doing things. "Oh...I see you both want to wear the red hat. I'll put on the timer for five minutes. When it rings it will be John's turn." Usually five minutes is enough for a child to feel he has had a good turn. Like the Taking Turns game described above, you can "teach" this method by "pretending" that two or more children want to play with the same thing and use the timer to give them each a turn. Be there to support and praise.

PRO-SOCIAL PLAY IDEAS

The idea here is to think of activities that are more fun to do with two or more people than alone. This gives you the opportunity to talk about how much fun it is to play with other people, and you are giving children easy success experiences while they gain experience with give and take. Here are some ideas for starters. You will think of many more.

Teach Names

Do all kinds of activities that involve children's names. Start by using children's names whenever you talk to them. This makes children feel valued and important, and also helps them learn the names of their friends so they can address them directly in friendly interactions. Some ideas:

- **Who is it?** Play guessing games with your pet puppet. Let the puppet describe various chilren in the group and let them guess who it is.

- **"Who's Here Today?"** Use photographs of children. You could put self-stick magnetic strips on the back of them and name and describe each child as a child puts them onto a metal surface.

- **Friends Gallery.** At home, a child could have a collection of pictures of his friends to play with and put on the refrigerator. Cover the photos with transparent self-adhesive paper and put a self-stick magnetic strip on the back.

- **Place Cards.** Make little "tent" place cards with children's photos on them. Cover them with transparent self-adhesive paper. When children help set the table, you can have them put out the place cards and name the child pictured.

- **Spotlight Dancers.** Play music and have everybody dance. Create a circle of light on the floor, or use a special rug. Call out children's names and let them get in the spotlight to dance. Everyone else could copy their actions.

Greeting Song

Have children sit in a circle (or a reasonable facsimile thereof). One child at a time jumps up and down in the middle of the circle as the others sing and clap:

Jerry's here today,
Jerry's here today,

We all clap together 'cause,
Jerry's here today.

Substitute each child's name, and sing to the tune of "Farmer in the Dell."

Pass the Teddy Bear (Or Anything Else) Game

Play some music, and have children pass a teddy bear from one to the other while the music is on. Turn off the music from time to time. When the music stops the child holding the teddy bear can do something special, like jump up and down. Vary the thing passed and what the child does when it's his "turn" to keep the game interesting.

Sing Together

Knowing the same songs makes children feel like they belong. Sing simple songs together each day. Likewise doing finger plays together like the "Eensie, Weensie Spider" or reciting poetry makes children feel like part of the gang. The "Toddler Stomp" activity in chapter 6 is another good prosocial activity.

Rituals in Routines

When everyone knows the cleanup song, or that when the big bell rings three times it's time to go in, or when a certain puppet comes out there will be a story, they will remind each other and cooperate eagerly.

Color Mixing Tube

Get about three feet of flexible, transparent plumbing tubing and push a cork into one end. With the child watching, fill the tube with water. Let the child pick two colors of food coloring you have available. Squirt one color into the open end of the tubing and then stick a second cork in. Now invert the

tube and remove the first
cork. Squirt the second color
in this end and replace the
cork. Invite two children to
tip the tube back and forth to
make the colors mix.

Rocking Boat

The popular "rocking boat"
that turns over into a set of
stairs is a good piece of
equipment for a toddler program, and it has the advantage of
multiple uses. It is safely built to be stable and when used as
a rocking boat it will not tip over. Children often will sing
"Row, row, row your boat" (or a version thereof) as they rock.
If only one child is in the rocking boat, nothing happens. It's
much more fun if two, three or four children are in it.

Ring Around the Rosie

Any simple circle game requires more than one person, and
this is the all-time favorite. The obvious appeal of this song is
falling down. And don't forget to put one child in the middle
to be the center of attention.

Follow the Leader

Toddlers are great at mimicking and it takes more than one
person to do this. The adult can designate which child will be
the leader, seeing that everybody gets a turn. Describe their
actions.

Ball Play

Rolling a ball back and forth is obviously more fun with two
or more children. Alone a child can roll or kick a ball and then
has to go and get it himself.

FREQUENTLY ASKED QUESTIONS

What do you do about the "bossy" child who always has to tell the others what to do?

Try to see what motivates the child to be bossy. Often this is the "born leader" – a child who has lots of good ideas and gets bored with just going with the flow. In order to have successful friendships, this child will need some good coaching from you in how to suggest things without being overbearing. Phrases like, "How about we..." and "I have a good idea...let's..." At the same time you'll coach the child to go along with the ideas of others some of the time. This is part of the progression from parallel play to associative, or more interactive play.

I have a child who always plays by himself and isn't interested at all in the other children. Should I be forcing him to play with the others?

Forcing is not the right word. Enticing is better. This child may simply not know how to enter a group of other children. Often it has to do with language development. If *you* choose to be a playmate of this child, and whenever you can, flop down and play with him, doing what he is doing and building on that, the other children will find the child more interesting and be drawn over to you. Then you can build bridges and help the children play together. Pick one of your more gregarious, easygoing children to play with the two of you, to increase the likelihood of success. Remember that social isolation can be a red flag, so don't ignore this isolated child.

CONCLUSION

"STARTING POINTS"

No book or collection of activities could ever give you all the ideas that might be useful about working with young children.

Use the ideas presented in this book as starting points for your own imagination and creative process. Make up your own variations, invent your own toys. Share your ideas and discoveries with others.

Keep learning. Attend conferences. Read. Take classes. Stay in touch with other early childhood professionals. Exchange ideas.

Most of all, have a wonderful time with the child or children in your care. There is nothing more exciting or more important than watching and participating in the growth of another human being. It is very hard work, but the rewards are immense!

APPENDIX

SAFETY POINTERS

Combine insatiable curiosity, a high activity level and relatively poor coordination and one realizes that toddlers can hurt themselves on just about anything. The fact that they put everything in their mouths makes choking a major safety concern as well. The most important safety device is close supervision by adults who are really paying attention. Listed here are some basic safety precautions, but don't limit yourself to these. Constantly be alert for any possibly hazardous situation.

INDOORS

• Make sure the environment is free of small objects children could choke on. Objects should be at least the size of a child's fist. Watch especially for toys of older children that may have small pieces dangerous to toddlers.

• Be especially alert for small sharp objects that could cause damage if swallowed, such as safety pins, staples, thumb tacks, paper clips, hair pins, chipped paint, nails, etc.

• Put safety plugs in all electrical outlets not in use. Extension cords are dangerous and should be used *only* for special occasions and under constant supervision. Use masking tape to secure to wall or floor.

• Make sure no appliance cords dangle down where children can pull on them.

• Put safety latches on low cabinet doors and drawers that might contain dangerous substances.

- Make sure toys are in good repair and that there are no sharp edges.

- Do not use glitter because it can scratch the cornea if the child rubs his eyes.

- Do not use balloons with toddlers because if the balloon breaks they can choke on pieces of rubber.

- Tack down loose carpets that could cause beginning walkers to trip and fall.

- Use furniture with rounded edges and maximum stability so that it cannot be tipped over if a child pulls up on it.

- Make sure wooden furniture and toys are free of splinters.

- Train staff and parents not to leave purses in places where children can get into them. They could contain potentially dangerous things such as medications or things to choke on.

- Store all medicine in a locked place totally inaccessible to children. Always keep medicine in original, labeled containers with childproof caps.

- Store all cleaning materials and poisonous substances in a locked cabinet, inaccessible to children. Purchase supplies with childproof tops.

- Post the poison control center phone number at all phones.

- Do not drink coffee or other hot beverages around children. Spilled hot liquids can cause third degree burns.

- Inspect water temperature from hot water faucets and adjust down if necessary. Water should not be warmer than 110 degrees.

- Encourage people to be careful when opening doors and discourage children from playing in front of doors.

- Be very careful when opening and closing doors to make sure no fingers get pinched. If possible, use guards on doors that prevent children from putting their fingers in the crack where they could get pinched.

- Tie cords from blinds or draperies high, out of reach of children.

- Never leave a child unattended on the changing table. In fact, it is good practice to have at least one hand on the child at all times.

- Keep diaper pails covered, and in a place that's inaccessible to babies.

- Check to make sure that any plants in the room are nontoxic, and keep them out of the reach of children.

- Keep cages of any classroom pets clean and the area around them free of debris. Only let children handle animals under the close supervision of an adult.

- Keep sharp objects like scissors and knives out of reach.

OUTDOORS

- Allow children to play only in a securely fenced-in area. The fence should be at least five feet high. The fence should go all the way down to the ground.

- Make sure the fence is in good repair with no gaps where it joins the gate or other places, or bulges at the bottom where children could squeeze through or get stuck.

- Make sure gate latches work well and are out of the reach of the children.

- If the fence is made of wood it should be sanded and free of splinters.

- Every time you go outside, check the ground and get rid of any debris or trash that may have blown in since the last time you were outside. Also get rid of natural materials such as acorns or small pine cones that children could choke on.

- Be sure there are no shrubs with thorns or poisonous berries.

- Cover your sand area completely with a sturdy weighted-down cover when not in use to keep out animals.

- Use shock absorbent materials under swings, slides, and climbing equipment to cushion possible falls. These soft surfaces should extend well beyond the equipment, as well as directly under it. The recommended depth depends on the material used (check child care licensing guidelines). Maintain at the proper depth.

- Supervise swings closely. Toddlers cannot predict the path of a swing and will walk right in front of it.

- Use sling type swings with soft seats or horizontal tire swings with toddlers.

- If possible, face slides away from the direct sun so they don't get too hot. Check the temperature of slides before letting children use them. Cool them down with water if necessary.

- Climbing structures should not be too high. Do not place a child on a climbing structure. They should be able to climb up themselves so that they can climb down themselves. Keep toddlers off of climbing equipment designed for older children.

- Check wooden equipment frequently for splinters and sand rough spots when necessary.

- Any gaps in climbers should be four inches or less, or larger than eight inches so the children cannot get their heads stuck in them. Vertical slats are more desirable than horizontal slats, because children always climb on horizontal slats. Any bolts on equipment should be smoothly rounded or recessed to prevent gouges. Make sure there are no sharp edges where children could get cut.

- Make sure there are no non-play hazards, such as electrical wires or exposed air conditioners or fuse boxes on the playground or that could be reached from climbing structures.

- Protect children's skin from over-exposure to the sun. Sunscreen, hats and bonnets are a good idea.

- Go inside when there is thunder and lightning.

- Do not use wading pools. Even toilet trained children may go to the bathroom in them. You may give each child a small tub or dishpan. Change the water for the next child's use.

- Maintain proper staff ratios at all times, inside and outside.

THESE SAFETY POINTERS ARE NOT MEANT TO BE EXHAUSTIVE. CHECK YOUR CHILD CARE LICENSING GUIDELINES FOR MORE DETAIL AND ADD ITEMS THAT ARE SPECIFIC TO YOUR OWN ENVIRONMENT.

INDEX

PART TWO — ACTIVITIES

CAUSE AND EFFECT

DRAMATIC PLAY

FREQUENTLY ASKED QUESTIONS

LANGUAGE DEVELOPMENT